EXETER MEDIEVAL ENGLISH TEXTS AND STUDIES

General Editors: Marion Glasscoe and M. J. Swanton

Julian of Norwich

A REVELATION OF LOVE

Edited by

MARION GLASSCOE

UNIVERSITY
of
EXETER
PRESS

First published by the University of Exeter 1976
Revised edition 1986, reprinted 1989
This revised edition 1993

University of Exeter Press
Reed Hall, Streatham Drive
Exeter, UK EX4 4QR

British Library Cataloguing in Publication Data

A catalogue record for this book is available from the
British Library

ISBN 0 85989 420 7

Typeset in 10pt Times by Kestrel Data, Exeter.

Printed in Great Britain by
BPCC Wheatons Ltd, Exeter.

CONTENTS

INTRODUCTION

1. The Author and the Manuscripts

In his introduction to the first printed edition of Julian's account of her revelations (1670) Serenus Cressy wrote:

> I was desirous to have told thee somewhat of the happy Virgin, the Compiler of these Revelations: But after all the search I could make, I could not discover any thing touching her, more than what she occasionally sprinkles in the Book itself.[1]

Knowledge of the details of the life of Julian of Norwich has increased little since then. She tells us that she received her visions during a serious illness when she was thirty and a half years old, in May 1373. This puts her date of birth in 1342. In 1394 Roger Reed, rector of St Michael Coslany, Norwich, bequeathed two shillings to Julian, anchorite,[2] and this would seem to establish her as a recluse by that date. Certainly she is mentioned by name as an anchoress at St Julian's church in Norwich in a will of 1404.[3] In 1413 the scribe of the shorter account of the revelations describes her as:

> A deuoute Woman and her Name is Iulyan that is recluse atte Norwyche and ʒitt on lyfe.[4]

Margery Kempe has left an interesting record of her visit to Julian about this time.[5] In 1416 Isabel Ufforde, Countess of Suffolk, left twenty shillings to Julian, recluse at Norwich.[6] A further will, which may possibly point to Julian's being alive in 1429, is that of Robert Baxster who in that year bequeathed three shillings and four pence to the anchorite in the church-yard of St Julian's Conesford in Norwich.[7] The advowson of St Julian's church was held by the Benedictine Priory at

Carrow. This connects Julian with the Benedictine tradition but there are no grounds for supposing that she was herself a Benedictine nun.

A record of Julian's revelations exists in two forms: 1, a shorter account to be found in British Library, Additional Manuscripts No. 33790; 2, a longer version three copies of which exist, Paris, Bibliothèque Nationale, Fonds Anglais No. 40 (to be abbreviated P), and British Library, Sloane Manuscripts No. 2499 and No. 3705 (to be abbreviated S1 and S2). It is generally agreed that the shorter version was written first and that the longer one takes into account Julian's growth in understanding of her revelations which, she tells us, took place for nearly twenty years after her initial experiencing of them.[8] This longer account thus refers to the years 1373 to 1393 and must postdate them, but beyond this there is no evidence of the actual date of composition.

The three manuscripts of the longer version were written in a later period than that to which they refer. P, written in a simplified bastard hand with some elements of italic style, is deliberately calligraphic and belongs to the late sixteenth or early seventeenth century. S1 and S2 in cursive hands belong respectively to the early and later seventeenth century.

It is possible that they were all connected with the work of the Benedictines of the counter-reformation who were active in reviving earlier modes of religious life. Augustine Baker, while he was spiritual director of the English Benedictine nuns in exile in Cambrai, wrote to his friend Sir Robert Cotton asking him for copies of the devotional works of the Medieval period:

> whereof though they have some, yet they want manie and thereuppon I am in their behalfe become an humble suitor vnto you, to bestowe on them such bookes as you please, either manuscript or printed being in English, conteining contemplation, Saints lives or other devotions.[9]

It is possible that P, with its beautifully executed calligraphic script and modernised readings, came to France, or was made there, for such nuns. Certainly Serenus Cressy, who worked on Baker's own manscripts and was a disciple of his, based his edition of Julian's text on this manuscript.

S1 has been chosen as copy text for this edition because its language is much closer to fourteenth-century English than that of P. It is sometimes messy and carelessly written, and it has some awkward but not impossible readings. There are glosses in the margin on some of the more archaic words, and passages to be noted are indicated there; both are added later and possibly in the same hand as that of the transcriber. It seems as if this was intended as a faithful copy of an earlier version; it could well have been used as the basis for such a manuscript as P. There are fifty-seven folio numbers added later but the pages are probably numbered by the original transcriber who duplicates the numbers 55 and 62, leaves 43v and 86v blank and unnumbered and arrives at a total of 110 pages. The manuscript has been subjected to a laminating process in restoration and it may well have been cropped at some time. In its present state it measures 12.4cm x 17.2cm; and there is no fly-leaf or title-page. There are no press marks earlier than those which refer to its place in Sloane's collection and, at the moment, there is no knowledge of how it got there. It is not easy to be sure about the relationship between P and S1. A collation of the two texts leads to the problem of whether they have a common source or represent two distinct manuscript traditions from a fifteenth or fourteenth-century original. Of the variations betwen them, some may be accounted for as simply editorial policy in the presentation of P, others to carelessness on the part of the scribe of one or other of the manuscripts, others remain inexplicable in these terms.

P frequently modernises readings in S1, eg.: *dwelleth* for *wonyth*, *verely* for *sekirly*, *great* for *mekil*, *drede* for *vggyng*, *undertake* for *underfongyn*, *continually monyng* for *swemefully*, etc. P also has passages which do not appear in S1. Often these do not make significant additions to the meaning, but act as a preface or summary to the thought of a related passage common to both manuscripts; or they expand and clarify the implications of a thought process which appears in a more compressed and awkward form in S1. Thus Julian explains that her reluctance to die arises not from fear,

> but it was to have lyved that I might have loved God better
> and longer tyme, that I might* have the more knoweing
> and lovyng of God in blisse of hevyn. (p. 4)

*P adds: *by the grace of that leuyng* etc. Or again, when Julian refers to her revelation of the crucified Christ as a source of strength in time of temptation, S1 reads:

> This I tooke for the time of my temptation etc. (p. 6)

P expands:

> Thus I toke it for that tyme that our lord Ihesu of his
> Curteys loue would shewe me comfort before the tyme of
> my temptation.

Some of these expansions are made at the expense of a prose rhythm which is more felicitous in S1. In chapter 7 S1 reads:

> our lord God shewed our lady Saint Mary in the same
> tyme; that is to mene (the) hey wisedom and trewth she
> had in beholding of hir maker* so grete, so hey, so mightie
> and so gode. This gretenes and this noblyth of the be-
> holdyng of God fulfilled her of reverend drede etc. (p. 10)

*P adds:

> This wysdom and truth · make her to beholde hyr god ·
> so gret etc.

The repeated construction in *this wysdom . . . made, this gretenes . . . fulfilled*, introduces an explanatory insistence which impedes the cadence of the reading in S1, where we move easily from the statement of what was seen to its inward effect.

Other passages present in P but not in S1 do add to the
meaning of the text but many of these may have been omitted
from S1 through natural scribal carelessness. In chapter 46 S1
reads:

> But our passand lif that we have here in our sensualite
> knowith not what ourself is;* than shal we verily and clerly
> sen and knowen our lord God in fulhede of ioy. (p. 64)

*P adds:

> but in our feyth · And whan we know and see verely and
> clerely what our selfe is ÷ than shalle etc.

Since the passage omitted ends with the same words as those
after which it started it is easy to see how the transcriber of
S1 might have left it out.[10] Conversely, of the few passages in
S1 which do not appear in P, a high proportion may be
accounted for on the same principle, homoeoteleuton, or on
those related to it.

There are however a residue of passages in both texts which
cannot be accounted for in this way. There are also significant
differences between the readings of single words in the two
manuscripts. Finally there are variations in chapter divisions.
On the whole, although the modernisation and possible
clarification of P blur the issues, it seems likely that S1 and P
relate to different originals.

S2 is much more obviously related to S1 than is P. It is
certainly modernised but it frequently has the same readings
as S1 where these differ from those in P. The chapter headings
too are common to these two manuscipts but do not appear
in P. However, differences between the two Sloane manuscripts indicate that their relationship is perhaps through a
common original rather than by direct copy.

2. The Text

The text of this edition is based on S1 and is conservative. The abbreviations in the manuscript, which are usual and need no comment, have been silently expanded, and obvious dittography has been emended without comment. The spacing of words in the manuscript is irregular; in this text compounds have generally been joined for the sake of clarity. Capitalisation in the manuscript is also irregular and this edition has its own system. The punctuation in S1 is loose and often difficult to determine because of the messy appearance of the manuscript. This edition has tried to preserve the sense indicated by what punctuation there is, but it is repunctuated in the interests of clarity and of the nature of Julian's book. (See below.)

Where the manuscript is not clear through omission of letters and sometimes, it would seem, whole words, emendations have been made in square brackets. These are based wherever possible on the earlier and more independent P, but in instances where the passage is in S1 but not in P, and in the chapter headings, S2 has been used. All emendations are accounted for in the notes. The more significant of the variations and additions in P have also been recorded in the notes, both because they sometimes clarify readings in S1 and for their intrinsic interest. Because of pressure on space those passages in P which simply expand without either clarifying or suggesting new meanings have been omitted.

Since the publication in 1670 of Cressy's edition of Julian's revelations as *XVI REVELATIONS of Divine Love, Shewed to a Devout Servant of our Lord, called MOTHER JULIANA* . . . , editions of the longer account have been titled *Revelations of Divine Love*. Julian herself, however, although she certainly talks of revelations in the plural, has a definite sense of them all combining into one total experience which she calls simply a revelation of love.

This is a revelation of love that Iesus Christ, our endless

blisse, made in xvi sheweings or revelations particular. (p.1)

In chapter 51 she talks of her gradual growth in understanding of the example of the lord and the servant as an integral part of her whole experience, and she refers to:

> the hole revelation from the begynnyng to the end, that is to sey, of this boke, which our lord God of his goodnes bryngeth oftentymes frely to the syte of myn vnder-stondyng. (p. 74)

When she reaches the account of the sixteenth and final shewing, she calls it:

> conclusion and confirmation of all xv. (p. 107)

This edition adopts for its title *A Revelation of Love* because that is what Julian calls her shewings and because it is felt that it more justly relates to her account of her experience.

This experience involves a special and direct knowledge of love, divine in origin but human in response, which, although it can thus be expressed in dual terms, is experienced as an indivisible unity which bridges the gap between God and man and gives a certainty of purpose to the failures and contradic-tions in human experience.

> 'I love thee and thou lovist me; and our love shal not be departid in two, and for thi profitt I suffre.' And all this was shewid in gostly vnderstondyng sayand these blissid words: 'I kepe the full sekerly.' (p. 131)

The above attempt to define the nature of Julian's experience is made possible precisely because of the quality which makes her so remarkable in the tradition of Christian mysticism to which she belongs: that is her use of language to approach directly that which is recognized as essentially ineffable. The church's account of mystical experience is that it is a mode of knowing which transcends the normal faculties of sense and intellect. It is a knowledge of God which is neither that of natural or dogmatic theology, although the discipline of both may prepare the way to it; it is a direct experience of God in the soul, at its profoundest level a transforming union. The literature of Christian mysticism which precedes, or is contemporary with Julian, is that of counsel on the contemplative discipline as preparation for such an experience, and of charting the nature of the physical, mental and spiritual experience which surrounds it. But the experience itself is recognized as being essentially non-verbal, expressible only in negatives or metaphors which lead to the silence of a different understanding.[11] The author of *The Cloud of Unknowing* talks of the contemplative discipline leading to

> a derknes, & as it were a cloude of vnknowyng, þou wost neuer what, sauyng þat þou felist in þi wille a nakid entent vnto God. þis derknes & þis cloude is, how-so-euer þou dost, bitwix þee & þi God, & letteþ þee þat þou maist not see him cleerly by liȝt of vnderstonding in þi reson, ne fele him in swetnes of loue in þin affecioun. & þerfore schap þee to bide in þis derknes as longe as þou maist, euermore criing after him þat þou louest; for ȝif euer schalt þou fele him or see him, as it may be here, it behoueþ alweis be in þis cloude & in þis derknes.

He continues that God is not to be reached in this experience by conscious intellect but,

> By loue may he be getyn & holden; bot bi þouȝt neiþer. & þerfore, þof al it be good sumtyme to þink of þe kyndnes & þe worþines of God in special, & þof al it be a liȝt & a party of contemplacioun: neuerþeles in þis werk it schal be casten down & keuerid wiþ a cloude of forȝetyng. & þou schalt step abouen it stalworþly, bot listely, wiþ a deuoute & a plesing stering of loue, & fonde for to peerse þat derknes abouen þee. & smyte apon þat þicke cloude of vnknowyng wiþ a scharp darte of longing loue, & go not þens for þing þat befalleþ.[12]

Paradoxically, the mystical experience which involves what is here called *unknowing* can bring overwhelming insight into the unity of all things in God. But it is an insight which resists verbal formulation. Isaac Luria, a mystic in a different tradition, that of Jewish Kabbalism in the sixteenth century, expresses the crux of the matter in a reply he is said to have given to an enquiry as to why he did not write down what he understood in a book:

> It is impossible, because all things are interrelated. I can hardly open my mouth to speak without feeling as though the sea has burst its dams and overflowed. How then shall I express what my soul has received, and how can I put it down in a book?[13]

It is just this gap between knowing and expressing that Julian tries to close. In so doing she makes at least something of her experience accessible to a wider circle of people than those already theologically or spiritually well equipped to understand her; she uses language with the quickening power of the artist through whom human experience is both interpreted and shared. It is precisely the overwhelming sense of the unity of experience in the reality of a divine purpose—a barrier to language for Luria—which informs Julian's prose. It is flexible to the pressure of exaltation, adoration, and excitement in understanding which it shapes; and the more convincingly for the moments of doubt, failure and outraged reason which it records as essential concomitants. Apart from the example of the lord and the servant, allegory and symbol are not used as means to express her spiritual apprehension. Images relating to Christ's passion are the mainspring of the revelations. For Julian the mystic, as for Langland the poet, it is the truth of the incarnation and passion that essentially gives meaning and value to human experience; it concerns the Word made flesh.

In her use of language Julian conveys an acute sense of the physical world—herrings' scales are simile for the spreading of blood from beneath the crown of thorns, the devil's face has the fierce intensity and colour of a newly fired brick—and an ability to delineate mental and spiritual experience. It is a language which expresses the emotions of faith but has a tough rational sub-structure to convey the illumination of understanding by that faith; both are part of a revelation of love.

> I had iii manner of vnderstonding in this light, charite: the first is charite onmade; the second is charite made; the iii is charite goven. Charite onmade is God; charite made is our soule in God; charite goven is vertue; and that is a precious geft of werking in which we loven God for himselfe and ourselves in God and that God loveth, for God. (p. 133)

This passage, like the tip of an iceberg, signals a deep supporting structure. It is an intellectual formulation in simply ordered prose which assimilates all Julian's growth in understanding of the nature of God and his relationship to his creation.

The unconventional punctuation of this edition, with its preference for semi-colons over full stops, is a deliberate attempt to clarify the movements of Julian's thought without disturbing too radically the essentially fluid nature of the linguistic structure in which each clause relates to the next to form intricate patterns of interdependency which it is difficult to break down into the more isolated units implied by formal grammatical sentences. It is no accident that Julian's favourite conjunction is *for*, with all its connotations of causal connection and purposeful action. A glance at chapter 49, pp. 69-70, will reveal that the second sentence runs for over half a page, expanding the implications of the initial assertion that our lif is all groundid and rotid in love to the point where the final statement can sensibly be made:

> we may not be blisfully save til we be verily in peace and in love; for that is our salvation.

However, the full theological implications of this whole passage, in turn, depend for their full meaning on Julian's explanation in the previous chapter of the psychological reality of this salvation as a resolution of the conflicts in man's nature.

An attempt has also been made not to disturb another feature of Julian's use of language: her tendency to ambiguities which coalesce two meanings and thus embody the unity of ex- perience that both point to.

> And the vertue of our lords word turnyth into the soule and quicknith the herte and entrith it by his grace into trew werkyng, and makyth it prayen wel blisfully and trewly to enioyen our lord; it is a ful blisful thankyng in his syte. (p. 58)

The phrase *blisfully and trewly* in its relation to *prayen* and *enioyen* has more than one possibility for the punctuator, depending on whether or not it is regarded as a single unit. This question in its turn cannot be separated from the decision as to how the final statement, *it is a ful blisful thankyng* etc., stands in relation to all that has gone before. The punctuation here allows for as many permutations of meaning as possible; for to pray well is truly and blissfully to enjoy our lord, and to enjoy our lord is to pray very blissfully and truly, and to enjoy him truly is to pray very blissfully, and all these activities are *a ful blisful thankyng in his syte*.

The complex nature of Julian's thought complicates gloss-ing. Two words have been omitted from the glossary both although, and precisely because, they are key words in the text: *kind* and *substance*. 'Kind' as a noun has its usual Middle English meaning of nature, natural order of things; as adjective it can be either natural, or, kind, compassionate. 'Substance' may be glossed as essential nature, core of reality. However both words depend on context for more accurate interpre-tation. Julian seems to imply that man's capacity for spiritual experience is what constitutes his substance as opposed to his more ephemeral sensuality, though both are united in God by virtue of the incarnation.

In our substance we arn full, and in our sensualite we

> faylyn; which faylyng God will restore and fulfill be
> werkyng mercy and grace plentiously flowand into us of
> his owne kynd godhede. (p. 91)

In the light of this understanding of substance and sensuality, kind takes on a variety of meanings which only context can define:

> for our kind which is the heyer part is knitt to God in the
> makyng; and God is knitt to our kinde which is the lower
> partie in our flesh takyng; and thus in Christ our ii kinds
> are onyd; for the Trinite is comprehendid [in] Criste in
> whome our heyer partie is groundid and rotid, and our
> lower partie the second person hath taken, which kynd
> first to him was adyte. (p. 92)

Moreover the two meanings of 'kind' as adjective may often coalesce. *Kynd godhede* in the first of the passages quoted above is one such example; in other contexts the double meaning illuminates and reinforces Julian's understanding that finally, *al shal be wel.* (p. 38)

> Our kindly will is to have God and the gode will of God
> is to have us. (p. 9)

Julian talks of herself as: a *simple creature that cowde no letter.* (p. 2) It is very probable that her account of the revelations was dictated to an amanuensis. Certainly the rhythms and inflexions of her use of language are often those of the speaking voice; moreover, the kind of rhetorical control shown in the passage quoted above (pp. 91-92), is quite consistent with an oral tradition. These factors, together with her manner of interrupting herself, as in the passage below, the frequent compression of structure in thought sequences, and the fact that the traditional formulations of the stages of mystical experience are not explicit in her account (although they operate silently as a frame of reference within which she must be understood), all point to an author thinking aloud rather than polishing pre- formulated ideas. The result is that the reader is involved in a primary mental process, and this in itself is an essentially creative element in the response evoked by Julian's account of her revelations.

Even while using it, Julian recognizes the final intractability of language as a medium for her understanding. Of the twelfth revelation she says:

> The nombre of the words passyth my witte and al my vnderstondyng and al my mights, and it arn the heyest, as to my syte; for therin is comprehendid—I cannot tellyn; but the ioy that I saw in the shewyng of them passyth al that herte may willen and soule may desire; and therefore the words be not declaryd here but every man after the grace that God gevyth him in vnderstondyng and lovyng receive hem in our lords menyng. (p. 37)

Julian talks of receiving her visions and her understanding of them in a sequence of time, but she shows that this process ultimately relates to a mode of being of a different order.

> I saw the soule so large as it were an endles world and as it were a blisfull kyngdom. (p. 109)

Similarly the reader, in his turn, is absorbed into a process of understanding which leads, not to a final intellectual formulation, but to a point where at least the possibility of a mode of knowing in which the *mene* of language has no place is glimpsed; in this book the words are only an approach to the meaning. However, the very process by which words are understood may act as a metaphor for the experience to which they relate.

> Words, after speech, reach
> Into the silence. Only by the form, the pattern,
> Can words or music reach
> The stillness.[14]

Julian's book is not a manual for contemplatives or a theological treatise, but she herself insists on her conformity to the teaching of the church[15] and her book can only properly be understood in its medieval context of such works. In fact they cross illuminate each other. Julian shows the teaching and the mystical theology of the medieval church, which condition her manner of thought and expression, alive in the working of her own experience. Her book suggests how the Christian mystic's experience of God, although it is not amenable to the normal faculties of consciousness, may still relate to, indeed be a necessary part of, man's total psychological integrity. Julian uses the language of orthodoxy, but with her the letter does not kill, it makes alive.

Exeter 1976   *Marion Glasscoe*

1 *XVI Revelations of Divine Love, Shewed to a Devout Servant of our Lord, called Mother Juliana An Anchorete of Norwich: Who lived in the Dayes of King Edward the Third.* ed. R. F. S. Cressy, London, 1670.
2 Norwich Consistory Court, 194, Harsyk.
3 Thomas Emund, Reg. Arunel, I. f. 540d (Lambeth Palace Library).
4 British Library, Additional Manuscripts No. 37790, f. 97.
5 *The Book of Margery Kempe.* ed. S. B. Meech & H. E. Allen, Early English Text Society, O. S. 212, 1940, p. 42.
6 Quoted in E. F. Jacob, *The Register of Henry Chichele*, 1938, pp. 94-95.
7 Norwich Consistory Court, 86, Surflete.
8 See p. 74.
9 British Library, Cotton Manuscripts, Julius C III, f. 12.
10 Cf. p. 2[1] & p. 138, 1, or p. 118[243] & p. 143, 243
11 Richard Rolle is an exceptional case here; he does express a lyrically poetic apprehension of God's love but he lacks the intellectual strength of writers like Hilton or the author of *The Cloud*, or Julian herslef.
12 *The Cloud of Unknowing.* ed. P. Hodgson, Early English Text Society, O. S. 218, 1944, pp. 16-17 & p. 26.

13 *Ta'alumōth Hokhmah. (Mysteries of Wisdom.)* Basle, 1629, 37b.
   Likkute Shas. (Comments on the Talmud.) Livorno, 1790, 33c.
   Paraphrased, G. G. Scholem, *Major Trends in Jewish Mysticism.*
   New York, 1941, p. 254
14 T. S. Eliot, 'Burnt Norton v', *Four Quartets*.
15 See p. 14.

SELECT BIBLIOGRAPHY

*This short bibliography is intended
only as an introduction to further study.*

EDITIONS AND TRANSLATIONS

Allen, H. E., ed., *English Writings of Richard Rolle*. Oxford, 1931. (Reprinted 1963.)

Beer, F., ed., *Julian of Norwich's Revelations of Divine Love*, Heidelberg, 1978. (Short Text).

Clark, J. P. H., and Dorward R., trans., *Walter Hilton: The Scale of Perfection*, New York, 1991.

Colledge, E., and Walsh, J., eds., *A Book of Showings to the Anchoress Julian of Norwich*, 2 Vols, Toronto, 1978. (Short and Long Texts).

Hodgson, P., ed., *The Cloud of Unknowing,* Early English Text Society, O.S. 218, London, 1944.

Meech, S. B. and Allen, H. E., ed., *The Book of Margery Kempe*. Early English Text Society, O. S. 212, London, 1940. (Reprinted 1961.)

Tolkein, J. R. R. ed., *Ancrene Wisse*. Early English Text Society, O. S. 249, London, 1962.

Underhill, E. trans., *The Scale of Perfection*. (Walter Hilton) London, 1923.

Windeatt, B. A., trans., *The Book of Margery Kempe*, Harmondsworth, 1985.

STUDIES

Butler, C. *Western Mysticism*. London, 1967.

Bynum, C W., *Jesus as Mother: Studies in the Spirituality of the High Middle Ages*, London, 1982.

Chambers, R. W. *On the Continuity of English Prose*. Early English Text Society, 191A, London, 1957.

Colledge, E. *The Medieval Mystics of England*. New York, 1961.

Davies, O., 'Transformational Processes in the Work of Julian of Norwich and Mechthild of Magdeburg' in *The Medieval Mystical*

Tradition in England V, ed. M. Glasscoe, Cambridge, 1992, pp 39-52.

Gillespie, V., and Ross, M., 'The Apophatic Image: The Poetics of Effacement in Julian of Norwich', in *The Medieval Mystical Tradition in England V*, ed. M. Glasscoe, Cambridge, 1992, pp. 53-77.

Glasscoe, M. 'Visions and Revisions: A Further Look at the Manuscripts of Julian of Norwich', *Studies in Bibliography*, 42 (1989), 103-20.

Glasscoe, M., *English Medieval Mystics: Games of Faith*, London, 1993.

Hodgson, P. 'Three Fourteenth-Century English Mystics', *Writers and their Work*, 196, London, 1967.

Jantzen, G., *Julian of Norwich*, London, 1987.

Johnston, W. *Silent Music*. New York, 1974.

Knowles, D. *The English Mystical Tradition*. London, 1962.

Lawlor, J. 'A Note on the *Revelations* of Julian of Norwich', *Review of English Studies*, N. S. 2 (1951) 255- 258.

Leclercq, J., *The Love of Learning and the Desire for God: A Study of Monastic Culture*, trans. C. Misrahi, New York, 1961.

Molinari, P. *Julian of Norwich. The Teaching of a Fourteenth- Century English Mystic*. London, 1958.

Park, T., 'Reflecting Christ: The Role of the Flesh in Walter Hilton and Julian of Norwich,' in *The Medieval Mystical Tradition in England V*, ed. M. Glasscoe, Cambridge, 1992, pp. 17-37.

Pelphrey, B., *Love was His Meaning: The Theology and Mysticism of Julian of Norwich*, Salzburg 1982.

Reynolds, A. M. 'Some Literary Influences in the *Revelations* of Julian of Norwich', *Leeds Studies in English and Kindred Languages*, Nos. 7-8 (1952) 18-28.

Smalley, B. *The Study of the Bible in the Middle Ages*. Oxford, 1952.

Stone, R. K. *Middle English Prose Style*. The Hague, 1970.

Tugwell, S., *Ways of Imperfection*, London, 1984.

Watson, N., 'The Trinitarian Hermeneutic in Julian of Noriwch's Revelation of Love', in *The Medieval Mystical Tradition in England V*, ed. M. Glasscoe, Cambridge, 1992, pp. 79-100.

Windeatt, B., 'Julian of Norwich and her Audience' *Review of English Studies*, n. s., 28 (1977), 1-17.

Windeatt, B., 'The Art of Mystical Loving', in *The Medieval Mystical Tradition in England I*, ed. M. Glasscoe, Exeter, 1980, pp 55-71.

Zeeman, E. 'Continuity in Middle English Devotional Prose', *Journal of English and Germanic Philology*, 55, (1956), 417-422.

TEXT

Revelations to one who could not read a letter.
Anno Domini, 1373.

1

A particular of the chapters.

The first chapter—off the noumber of the revelations par-
ticularly. This is a revelation of love that Iesus Christ, our
endless blisse, made in xvi sheweings or revelations particular;
off the which the first is of his pretious coroning with thornys;
and therewith was comprehended and specifyed the Trinite
with the incarnation and unite betwix God and man soule,
with many faire sheweings of endless wisedome and teacheing
of love, in which all the sheweings that follow be grounded
and onyd. The iid is the discolloureing of his faire face in
tokenyng of his deareworthy passion. The iiid is that our lord
God, almighty wisedome, all love, right as verily as he hath
made every thing that is, also verily he doith and workeith all
thing that is done. The iiiith is the scourgeing of his tender
body with plentious sheddying of his blood. The vth is that
the fend is overcome by the pretious passion of Christe. The
vi is the worshippfull thankeing of our lord God in which he
rewardeth his blissed servants in hevyn. The vii is often
feeleing of wele and wo—feleing of wele is gracious touching
and lightening, with trew sekirness of endless ioy; the feleing
of wo is temptation be heavyness and irkehede of our fleshly
liveing—with ghostly understanding that we arn kept aso
sekirly in love, in wo as in wele, be the godeness of God. The
viii is the last paynes of Christ and his cruelle dyeing. The ix
is of the likeing which is in the blissefull Trinite of the herde
passion of Christe and his rewfull dyeing; in which ioy and
likeing he will wee be solacid and myrthid with him till whan
we come to the fullhede in heavyn. The xth is our lord Iesus
shewith in love his blissefull herte even cloven on two

1

enioyand. The xi is an hey ghostly sheweing of his deareworthy
moder. The xii is that our lord is most worthy being. The xiii
is that our lord God wil we have gret regard to all the deeds
that he hath done in the gret nobleth of all things makying,
and of the excellency of man makeyng, which is above all his
workes, and of the pretious asseth that he hath made for man
synne, turneing all our blame into endlesse worshippe; where
also our lord seith: 'Behold and see;[1] for be the same mightie
wisedome and goodnesse I shall make w[e]le[2] all that is not
wele and thou shalt see it.' And in this he will we keepe us
in the feith and trowthe of holy church, not willing to wete his
privityes now, but as it longyth to us in this life. The xiiii is
that our lord is ground of our beseekeing. Herein were seene
ii properties: that one is rightfull prayer, that other is sekir
truste, which he will both be alike large; and thus our prayers
likyth him and he of his goodnesse fullfilleth it. The xvth, that
we shall sodenly be taken from al our peyne and from all our
wo and, of his goodnesse, we shall come up aboven where we
shall have our lord Iesus to our mede and be fullfilled of ioy
and blisse in hevyn. The xvi is that the blissefull Trinite our
maker, in Christe Iesus our saviour, endlessely wonyth in our
soule, worshipfully reuland and geveand all things, us mightily
and wisely saveand and keepeand for love, and we shall not
be overcome of our enemy.

2

*The ii chapter—of the tyme of these revelations, and how she
asked iii petitions.*

These revelations were shewed to a simple creature that cowde
no letter, the yeere of our lord 1373, the viiith[3] day of May;
which creature desired afore iii gifts of God: the first was
mende of his passion, the ii was bodily sekenesse in youth at
xxx yeeres of age, the iii was to have of Gods gift iii wounds.
As in the first methought I had sume feleing in the passion
of Christe, but yet I desired more be the grace of God.

2

Methought I would have beene that time with Mary Magdalen and with other that were Crists lovers, and therefore I desired a bodily sight wherein I might have more knowledge of the bodily peynes of our saviour, and of the compassion [of][4] our lady and of all his trew lovers that seene that time his peynes, for I would be one of them and suffer with him. Other sight ner sheweing of God desired I never none till the soule was departid fro the body. The cause of this petition was that after the sheweing I should have the more trew minde in the passion of Christe. The iid came to my mynde with contrition, frely desireing that sekenesse so herde as to deth that I might, in that sekeness, vnderfongyn all my rites of holy church, myselfe weneing that I should dye, and that all creatures might suppose the same that seyen me; for I would have no manner comfort of eardtly life. In this sikenesse I desired to have all manier peynes bodily and ghostly that I should have if I should dye, with all the dreds and tempests of the fends, except the outpassing of the soule. And this I ment for I would be purged be the mercy of God and after lyven more to the worshippe of God because of that sekenesse; and that for the more speede in my deth, for I desired to be soone with my God. These ii desires of the passion and the sekenesse I desired with a condition,[5] sey[ing][6] thus: 'Lord, thou wotith what I would—if it be thy will that I have it; and if it be not thy will, good lord, be not displeased, for I will nought but as thou wilt.' For the iii, by the grace of God and teachyng of holy church, I conceived a mighty desire to receive iii wounds in my life: that is to sey the wound of very contrition, the wound of kinde compassion and the wound of willfull longing to God. And all this last petition I asked without any condition. These ii desires foresaid passid fro my minde, and the iiid dwelled with me continually.

3

Of the sekenese opteyned of God be petition—iii chapter.

And when I was thirty yers old and halfe God sent me a bodely sekeness in which I lay iii dayes and iii nights; and on the fourth night I tooke all my rites of holy church and wened not a levyd till day. And after this I langorid forth ii dayes and ii nights. And on the iii night I wened oftentimes to have passyd, and so wened they that were with me. And in youngith yet, I thought great sweeme to dye; but for nothing [that]⁷ was in earth that me lekid to levin for, ne for no peyne that I was aferd of, for I trusted in God of his mercy; but it was to have lyved that I might have loved God better and longer tyme, that I might have the more knoweing and lovyng of God in blisse of hevyn. For methought all the time that I had lived here, so little and so short in reward of that endlesse blisse—I thought nothing. Wherefore I thought: 'Good lord, may my living no longer be to thy worshippe!' And I understood by my reason and be my feleing of my peynes that I should dye. And I assented fully with all, with all the will of my herte, to be at God will. Thus I durid till day, and be than my body was dede fro the middis downewards as to my feleing. Then was I stered to be sett upright, underlenand with helpe, for to have more fredam of my herte to be at Gods will, and thinkeing on God while my life would lest. My curate was sent for to be at me endeing, and by than he cam I had sett my eyen and might not speke. He sett the cross before my face and seid: 'I have browte thee the image of thy maker and saviour. Louke thereupon and comfort thee therewith.' Methought I was wele, for my eyen were sett uprightward into hevyn where I trusted to come be the mercy of God. But nevertheless I assented to sett my eyen in the face of the crucifix if I might, and so I dede, for methought I might longer duren to loke evenforth than right up. After this my sight began to failen and it was all derke about me in the chamber

4

as it had be night, save in the image of the cross wherein I beheld a comon light, and I wiste not how. All that was beside the cross was uggely to me as if it had be mekil occupied with the fends. After this the other party of my body began to dyen so ferforth that onethys I had ony feleing, with shortness of onde. And than I went sothly to have passid. And, in this, sodenly all my peyne was taken fro me and I was as hele, and namely in the other party of my body, as ever I was aforn. I mervalid at this soden change for methought it was a privy workeing of God and not of kinde. And yet by the feleing of this ease I trusted never the more to levyn; ne the feleing of this ease was no full ease to me, for methought I had lever a be deliveryd of this world. Than came suddenly to my minde that I should desyre the second wounde, of our lords gracious gift, that my body might be fullfilled with minde and felying of his blissid passion; for I would that his peynes were my peynes with compassion, and afterward longeing to God. But in this I desired never bodily sight nor sheweing of God, but compassion, as a kinde soule might have with our lord Iesus, that for love would beene a dedely man; and therefore I desired to suffer with him.

4

Here begynnith the first revelation of the pretious crownyng of Christe etc. in the first chapter; and how God fullfilleth the herrte with most ioy, and of his greate meekenesse, and how the syght of the passion of Criste is sufficient strength ageyn all temptations of the fends, and of the gret excellency and mekenesse of the blissid virgin Mary—the iiii chapter.

In this sodenly I saw the rede blode trekelyn downe fro under the garlande, hote and freisly and ryth plenteously, as it were in the time of his passion that the garlande of thornys was pressid on his blissid hede, ryte so both God and man, the same that sufferd thus for me. I conceived treuly and mightily that it was himselfe shewed it me without ony mene. And in

5

the same sheweing sodenly the Trinite fullfilled the herte most of ioy. And so I understood it shall be in hevyn withoute end to all that shall come there. For the Trinite is God, God is the Trinite; the Trinite is our maker and keeper, the Trinite is our everlasting lover, everlasting ioy and blisse, be our lord Iesus Christ. And this was shewed in the first and in all; for where Iesus appereith the blissid Trinite is understond, as to my sight. And I said: 'Benedicite domine!' This I said, for reverence in my meneing, with a mighty voice; and full gretly was astonyed for wonder and mervel that I had that he that is so reverend and dredfull will be so homely with a synfull creture liveing in wretched flesh.[8] This I tooke for the time of my temptation, for methowte by the sufferance of God, I should be tempted of fends or I dyed. With this sight of the blissid passion with the Godhede that I saw in myne understonding, I knew wele that it was strength enow to me, ya and to all creturers leving, ageyn all the fends of hell and ghostly temptation. In this he browght our blissid lady to my understonding. I saw hir ghostly in bodily likeness, a simple mayde and a meke, young of age and little waxen above a child, in the stature that she was wan she conceived with child. Also God shewid in party the wisedam and the trueth of hir soule, wherein I understood the reverend beholding that she beheld hir God and maker, mervelyng with great reverence that he would be borne of hir that was a simple creature of his makeyng. And this wisdam and trueth, knowyng the greteness of [her][9] maker and the littlehede of hirselfe that is made, caused hir sey full mekely to Gabriel: 'Lo me, Gods handmayd.' In this sight I undestoode sothly that she is mare than all that God made beneath hir in worthyness and grace; for aboven hir is nothing that is made but the blissid [manhood][10] of Christe, as to my sight.

5

How God is to us everything that is gode, tenderly wrappand us; and all thing that is made, in regard to almighty God, it is nothing; and how man hath no rest till he nowteth himselfe and all thing for the love of God—the v chapter.

In this same time our lord shewed to me a ghostly sight of his homely loveing. I saw that he is to us everything that is good and comfortable for us. He is our clotheing that for love wrappith us, [halseth][11] us and all beclosyth us for tender love, that hee may never leave us, being to us althing that is gode, as to myne understondyng. Also in this he shewed a littil thing, the quantitye of an hesil nutt in the palme of my hand; and it was as round as a balle. I lokid thereupon with eye of my understondyng and thowte: 'What may this be?' And it was generally answered thus: 'It is all that is made.' I mervellid how it might lesten, for methowte it might suddenly have fallen to nowte for littil. And I was answered in my understondyng: 'It lesteth and ever shall, for God loveth it; and so allthing hath the being be the love of God.' In this littil thing I saw iii properties: the first is that God made it, the second is that God loveth it, the iiid, that God kepith it. But what is to me sothly the maker, the keper, and the lover I canot tell; for, till I am substantially onyd to him, I may never have full rest ne very blisse; that is to sey, that I be so festined to him that there is right nowte that is made betwix my God and me. It needyth us to have knoweing of the littlehede of creatures and to nowtyn all thing that is made for to love and have God that is unmade. For this is the cause why we be not all in ease of herete and soule: for we sekyn here rest in these things that is so littil, wherin is no rest, and know not our God that is almighty, al wise, all gode; for he is the very rest. God will be knowen, and him liketh that we rest in him; for all that is beneth him sufficeth not us; and this is the cause why that no soule is restid till it is nowted of all things that is made. Whan he is willfully nowtid, for love to have him that is all, then is he abyl to receive ghostly rest. Also our lord God shewed that it is full gret plesance to him that a sily soule come to him nakidly and pleynly and homely. For this is the kinde yernings[12] of the soule by the touching of the Holy Ghost, as be the understondyng that I have in this sheweing: 'God, of thy

7

goodnesse, give me thyselfe; for thou art enow to me and I may nothing aske that is less that may be full worshippe to thee. And if I aske anything that is lesse, ever me wantith, but only in thee I have all.' And these words arn full lovesome to the soule and full nere touchen the will of God and his goodness; for his goodness comprehendith all his creatures and all his blissid works, and overpassith without end, for he is the endleshede. And he hath made us only to himselfe and restorid us be his blissid passion and kepith us in his blissid love. And all this is of his goodness.

6

How we shold pray, of the gret tender love that our lord hath to mannes soule willing us to be occupied in knowing and loveing of him—the vi chapter.

This sheweing was made to lerne our soule wisely to clevyn to the goodnes of God. And in that time the custome of our prayeing was browte to mende: how we use, for lak of understondyng and knowing of love, to make many menys. Than saw I sothly that is more worshippe to God, and more very delite, that we faithfully pray to himselfe of his goodness and clevyn thereto be his grace, with trew understondyng and stedfast be love, than if we made all the menys that herte can thinke; for if we make all these menys, it is to litil and not full worshippe to God, but in his goodnes is all the hole, and there failith right nowte. For thus, as I shall say, came to my minde in the same time: we pray to God for his holy flesh and for his pretious blode, his holy passion, his deareworthy death and wounds, and all the blissid kindenes, the endles life, that we have of all this is his goodnes; and we pray him for his sweete moder love that him bare, and all the helpe we have of her is of his [g]odeness;[13] and we pray by his holy cross that he dyed on, and all the vertue and the helpe that we have of the cross, it is of his godeness. And on the same wise, all the helpe that we have of special saints and all the blissed

8

company of hevyn, the dereworthy love and endles freind-
shippe that we have of them, it is of his godenes; for God of
his godenes hath ordeyned meanys to helpe us, wole faire and
fele, of which the chiefe and principal mene is the blissid kinde
that he toke of the mayd, with all the menys that gone aforn
and cum after which belongyn to our redemption and to
endless salvation. Wherefore it pleaseth him that we seke him
and worship be menys, understondyng and knoweing that he
is the goodness of all; for the goodness of God is the heyest
prayer and it comith downe to the lowest party of our nede.
It quickyth our soule and bringith it on life and makyth it for
to waxen in grace and vertue. It is nerest in kind and ridiest
in grace; for it is the same grace that the soule sekith, and evir
shall, till we know[14] verily that hath us all in himselfe
beclosyd;[15] for he hath no dispite of that he hath made, ne he
hath no disdeyne to serve us at the simplest office that [t]o[16]
our body longyth in kinde, for love of the soule that he hath
made to his owne likness; for as the body is cladde in the cloth,
and the flesh in the skyne, and the bonys in the flesh, and the
herte in the bouke, so arn we, soule and body, cladde in the
goodnes of God and inclosyd; ya, and more homley, for all
these may wasten and weren away; the godenes of God is ever
hole, and more nere to us withoute any likenes; for treuly our
lover desireth that our soule cleve to hym with all the might
and that we be evermore clevand to his godenes; for of all
thing that herete may thinke, it plesyth most God and sonest
spedyth; for our soule is so specially lovid of him that is heiest
that it overpassyth the knoweing of all creatures—that is to
seyen, there is no creature that is made that may wetyn how
mekyl and how swetely and how tenderly our maker loveth
us. And therefore we may with his grace and his helpe stond
in ghostly beholding, with everlestyng merveyling in this hey,
overpassing, onenestimable love that almitie God hath to us
of his godenes. And therefore we may aske of our lover with
reverence all that we willen; for our kindly will is to have God
and the gode will of God is to have us. And we may never
blyn of willing ne of longyng till we have him in fullhede of
ioy, and than may we no more willen; for he will that we by

9

occupyed in knoweing and loveing til the tyme that we shall
be fulfilled in hevyn. And therefore was this lesson of love
shewid, with all that followith, as ye shall se; for the strength
and the ground of all was shewed in the first sight; for of all
thing, the beholding and the lovyng of the maker makith the
soule to seeme lest in his owne sight, and most fillith it with
reverend drede and trew mekenes, with plenty of charitie to
his even cristen.

7

*How our lady, beholdyng the gretenes of hir maker, thowte
hirselfe leste, and of the great droppys of blode renning from
under the garland, and how the most ioy to man is that God
most hie and mightie is holyest and curtesiest—vii chapter.*

And to lerne us this, as to myne understondyng, our lord God
shewed our lady Saint Mary in the same tyme; that is to mene
[the][17] hey wisedome and trewth she had in beholding of hir
maker so grete, so hey, so mightie and so gode. This gretenes
and this noblyth of the beholdyng of God fulfilled her of
reverend drede, and with this she saw hirselfe so litil and so
low, so simple and so pore, in reward of hir lord God, that
this reverend drede fulfillid hir of mekenes. And thus, by this
grounde, she was fulfillid of grace and of al manner of vertues
and overpassyth all creatures. In all the tyme that he shewed
this that I have said now in ghostly sight, I saw the bodyly
sight lesting of the plentious bledeing of the hede. The grete
dropis of blode fel downe from under the garland like pellots
semand as it had cum out of the veynis; and in the comeing
out it were browne rede, for the blode was full thick; and in
the spredeing abrode it were bright rede; and whan it come
to the browes, than it vanyshid; notwithstondyng the bleding
continuid till many things were seene and understondyn. The
fairehede and the livelyhede is like nothing but the same. The
plentioushede is like to the dropys of water that fallen of the
evys after a greate showre of reyne that fall so thick that no

10

man may numbre them with bodily witte. And for the
roundhede, it were like to the scale of heryng in the spreadeing
on the forehead. These iii come to my [mynde][18] in the tyme:
pellots, for roundhede, in the comynge out of the blode; the
scale of herying, in the spreadeing in the forehede, for
roundhede; the dropys of evese, for the plentioushede in-
umberable. This shewing was quick and lively, and hidouse
and dredfull, swete and lovely. And of all the sight it was most
comfort to me that our God and lord, that is so reverent and
dredefull, is so homley and curtes. And this most fullfilled me
with likeing and sekirnes of soule. And to the understondyng
of this he shewid this opyn example: it is the most worshippe
that a solemne king or a grete lord may doe a pore servant if
he will be homely with him, and namely if he shewith it
himselfe, of a full trew meneing and with a glad cheere, both
prive and partie. Than thinkyth this pore creature thus: 'A!
What might this nobil lord doe more worshipp and ioy to me
than to shew me, that am so simple, this mervelous homlyhede? Sothly it is more ioy and likeing to me than he gave
me grete gifts and were himselfe strange in maner.' This bodily
example was shewid so hey that manys herete might be
ravishid and almost forgettyng himselfe for ioy of this grete
homlyhede. Thus it fareith be our lord Iesus and be us; for
sothly it is the most ioy that may be, as to my sight, that he
that is heyest and migtyest, noblest and worthyest, is lowest
and mekest, homlyest and curteysest. And treuly and sothly
this mervelous ioy shall be shewne us all whan we se him; and
this will our lord, that we willen and trowen, ioyen and liken,
comfortyn us and solacyn us, as we may, with his grace and
with his helpe, into the tyme that we se it verily; for the most
fulhede of ioy that we shal have, as to my sight, is the
mervelous curtesie and homlyhede of our fader that is our
maker, in our lord Iesus Criste that is our brother and our
saviour. But this mervelous homlyhede may no man weten in
this tyme of life, but he have it of special shewing of our lord,
or of grete plenty of grace inwardly govyn of the Holy Ghost.
But faith and beleve with charite deservith the mede, and so
it is had be grace; for in faith with hope and charete our life

11

is groundyd. The shewyng, made to whome that God will, pleynly techith the same, openyd and declarid with many privy points longing to our faith which be worshipfull to knowen. And whan the shewyng, which is goven in a tyme, is passyd and hid, than the feith kepyth be grace of the Holy Ghost into our life end. And thus be the shewyng it is not other than the faith, ne less ne more, as it may be seene be our lords meneing in the same matter be than it come to the end.

8

A recapitulation of that is seid and how it was shewid to hir generally for all—viii chapter.

And as longe as I saw this sight of the plentious bleding of the hede I might never stinte of these words: 'Benedicite domine!'. In which sheweyng I understode vi things: the first is the toknys of the blissid passion and the plentious sheddyng of his pretious blode; the iid is the maiden that is derworthy moder; the iiid is the blissfull Godhede that ever was, is and ever shal bene, al mighty, al wisdam, al love; the iiiith is althing that he hath hath made; for wele I wete that hevyn and erth and all that is made is mekil and large, faire and gode, but the cause why it is shewid so litil to my sight was for I saw it in the presence of him that is the maker of all thing, for a soule that seith the maker of all, all that is made semith full litil; the vth is he that made all things for love; be the same love it is kept and shall be withoute end; the vith is that God is al thing that is gode, as to my sight, and the godenes that al thing hath, it is he; and al these our lord shewid me in the first sight with time and space to beholden it. And the bodily sight stinted and the gostly sight dwellid in myne understondyng. And I abode with reverent drede ioyand in that I saw. And I desired as I durst to se more, if it were his will, or ell lenger time the same. In al this I was mekil sterid in charite to mine even cristen, that thei might seen and knowyn the same that I saw; for I would it were comfort to they, for al

12

this sight was shewid general. Than said I to them that were aboute me: 'It is today domysday with me.' And this I said for I went a deid; for that day that a man deith he is demyd as he shal be without end, as to my understondyng. This I seid for I would thei lovid God the better, for to make hem to have mende that this life is shorte as thei might se in example; for in al this time I went have deid and that was mervil to me and sweeme in partie, for methowte this vision was shewid for hem that should leven. And that I say of me I sey in the person of al myn even cristen, for I am lernyd in the gostly shewing of our lord God that he menyth so; and therefore I pray you al for Gods sake and counsel you for your owne profitt that ye levyn the beholding of a wretch that it was shewid to, and mightily, wisely and mekely behold God, that of his curtes love and endles godenes wolde shewyn it generally in comfort of us al; for it is Gods will that ye take it with gret ioy and likyng as Iesus had shewid it on to you all.

9

Of the mekenes of this woman kepeing hir alway in the feith of holy church, and how he that lovyth his evyn cristen for God lovith allthing—ix chapter.

For the shewing I am not goode but if I love God the better; and in as much as ye love God the better it is more to you than to me. I sey not this to hem that be wise, for thei wote it wele; but I sey it to yow that be simple for ese and comfort, for we arn al one in comfort; for sothly it was not shewid me that God lovid me better than the lest soule that is in grace, for I am sekir that there be many that never had shewing ner sight, but of the comon techyng of holy church, that loven God better than I; for if I loke singularly to myselfe I am right nowte; but in general I am in hope, in onehede of charitie with al myn evyn cristen; for in this onehede stond the life of all mankinde that shall be savid; for God is all that is good, on to my sight, and God hat made al that is made, and God

lovith al that he hath made, and he that generaly loveith al
his evyn cristen for God, he lovith al that is; for in mankynd
that shall be savid is comprehendid al: that is to sey, all that
is made and the maker of al; for in man is God, and God is
in al. And I hope be the grace of God he that beholdith it
thus shal be truely taught and mightily comforted if he nedith
comforte. I speake of hem that shal be save, for in this time
God shewid me none other. But in althing I leve as holy church
levith, preachith and teachith; for the feith of holy church the
which I had aforn hand understonden and, as I hope, by the
grace of God wilfully kept in use and custome, stode continualy in my sight, willing and meneing never to receive
onything that might be contrary therunto. And with this entent
I beheld the shewing with al my diligens; for in al this blissid
shewing I beheld it as one in Gods meneyng. All this was
shewid by thre: that is to sey, be bodily sight and by word
formyd in my understonding and be gostly sight. But the gostly
sight I cannot ne may not shew it as hopinly ne as fully as I
wolde. But I truste in our lord God almightie that he shal of
his godenes, and for yowr love, make yow to take it more
gostly and more swetely than I can or may telle it.

10

*The iid revelation is of his discolouryng etc., of our redemption,
and the discolouring of the vernacle, and how it plesith God
we seke him besily, abiding him stedfastly and trusting hym
mightily—x chapter.*

And after this I saw with bodily sight in the face of the crucifix
that henge before me, in the which I behelde continualy, a
parte of his passion: despite, spitting and sollowing and
buffetting and many langoryng peynes, mo than I can tel, and
often changing of colour. And one time I saw how halfe the
face, begyning at the ere, overrede[19] with drie blode til it
beclosid to the mid face, and after that, the tuther halfe
beclosyd on the same wise, and therewhiles in this party even

14

as it came. This saw I bodily, swemely and derkely, and I desired more bodily sight to have sene more clerely. And I was answered in my reason: 'If God wil shew thee more, he shal be thy light. Thee nedith none but him.' For I saw him [and sought hym];[20] for we arn now so blynd and so unwise that we never sekyn God til he of his godenes shewith him to us; and we ought se of him graciously, than arn we sterid by the same grace to sekyn with gret desire to se him more blisfully; and thus I saw him and sowte him, and I had him and I wantid hym. And this is, and should be, our comon werkeyng in this,[21] as to my sight. One tyme mine understondyng was led downe into the see-ground, and there I saw hill and dalis grene, semand as it were mosse begrowne, with wrekke and gravel. Than I understode thus: that if a man or a woman were under the broade watyr, if he might have sight of God so, as God is with a man continually, he should be save in body and soule and take no harme and, overpassing, he should have mor solace and comfort than al this world can telle; for he wille that we levyn that we se him continualy, thowe that us thinkeith that it be but litil, and in this beleve he makith us evermore to getyn grace; for he will be sene and he wil be sowte; he wil be abedyn and he wil be trosted. This iid sheweing was so low and so litil and so simple that my sprets were in grete travel in the beholding, mornand, dredfull and longand; for I was sumtime in doute whither it was a shewing. And than divers times our gode lord gave me more sight whereby I understode treuly that it was a shewing. It was a figure and likenes of our foule dede hame that our faire, bright, blissid lord bare for our sins. It made me to thinke of the holy vernacle of Rome which he hath portrayed with his owne blissid face when he was in his herd passion, wilfully going to his deth, and often chongyng of colour. Of the brownehede and blakehede, reulihede and lenehede of this image, many mervel how it might be, stondyng he portraied it with his blissid face which is the fairhede of heavyn, flowre of erth and the fruite of the mayden wombe. Than how might this image be so discolouring and so fer fro faire? I desire to sey like as I have understond be the grace of God. We know in our faith and beleve be the teaching and preching of holy church that the blissed Trinite made mankinde to his image and to his likenes. In the same maner wise we knowen that whan man felle so deepe and so wretchidly be syne there was none other helpe to restore man but throw him that made man. And that made man for love, be the same love he would restore man to the same blisse, and overpassing. And like as we were like made to the Trinite in our first makyng, our maker would that we should be like Iesus Criste our saviour, in hevyn without ende, be the vertue of our geynmakyng. Than atwix these two he would, for love and worshippe of man, make himselfe as like to man in this dedely life, in our foulehede and our wratchidnes, as man myght be without gilte. Whereof it meneith as it was aforseyd: it was the image and likenes of our foule blak dede hame wherein our faire, bryte, blissid lord God is hid. But ful sekirly I dar sey, and we owen to trowen, that so faire a man was never none but he till what tyme his faire colour was chongyd with travel and sorrow and passion, deyeng. Of this it is spoken in the viii revelation where it tretith more of the same likenes. And there it seith of the vernacle of Rome, it mevyth be dyvers chongyng of colour and chere, sometyme more comfortably and lively, and some-time more reuly and dedely, as it may be seene in the viii revelation. And this vision was a lernyng to myn vnder-stondyng that the continual sekyng of the soule plesith God ful mekyl; for it may do no more than sekyn, suffrin and trosten, and this [is][22] wrought in the soule that hath it be the Holy Ghost; and the clernes of fyndyng is of his special grace whan it is his will. The sekyng with feith, hope and charite plesyth our lord, and the finding plesyth the soule and fulfillith it with ioy. And thus was I lernyd to myn vnderstondyng that sekyng is as good as beholdyng for the tyme that he will suffer the soule to be in travel. It is God wille that we seke him to the beholdyng of him, for be that he shall shew us himselfe of his special grace whan he wil. And how a soule shall have him in his beholdyng he shal teche himselfe; and that is most worshipp to him and profitt to thyselfe, and most receivith of mekenes and vertues with the grace and ledyng of the Holy

16

Goste; for a soule that only festinith him on to God with very troste, either be sekyng or in beholdyng, it is the most worshipp that he may don to him, as to my sight. These arn two werkyng that mown be seene in this vision: that on is sekyng, the other is beholdyng. The sekyng is common; that, every soule may have with his grace, and owith to have that discretion and techyng of the holy church. It is God wil that we have thre things in our sekyng: the first is that we sekyn wilfully and bisily, withouten slauth, as it may be throw his grace, gladly and merili withoute onskilful hevynes and veyne sorow; the second is that we abide him stedfastly for his love, withoute gruching and striveing ageyns him, in our lives end, for it shall lesten but awhile; the thred that we trosten in him mightily of fulsekird feith, for it is his wil. We knowen he shall appere sodenly and blisfully to al his lovers; for his werkyng is privy, and he wil be perceivid, and his appering shal be swith sodeyn, and he wil be trowid, for he is full hend and homley—blissid mot he ben!

11

The iiid revelation etc, how God doth althing except synne, never chongyng his purpose without end, for he hath made althing in fulhede of goodnes—xi chapter.

And after this I saw God in a poynte, that is to sey, in myn vnderstondyng, be which sight I saw that he is in al things. I beheld with avisement, seing and knowing in sight with a soft drede, and thought: 'What is synne?' for I saw truly that God doth althing be it never so litil. And I saw truly that nothing is done be happe ne be aventure, but althing be the foreseing wisedome of God. If it be happe or adventure in the sight of man, our blindhede and our onforesight is the cause, for the things that arn in the foreseing wisdam of God fro without beginning (which rightfully and worshippfully and continualy he ledyth to the best end as they comen aboute) fallyn to us sodenly, ourselfe unwetyng; and thus, be our blindhede and

17

our onforsighte, we seyen these ben happis and aventures; but to our lord God thei be not so. Wherefore me behovith nedes to grant that althing that is done, it is wel done, for our lord God doth alle; for in this time the werkyng of cretures was not shewid, but of our lord God in the creature; for he is in the mydde poynt of allthyng and all he doith, and I was sekir he doith no synne. And here I saw sothly that synne is no dede, for in al this was not synne shewid. And I wold no lenger mervel in this, but beheld our lord, what he wold shewen. And thus, as it might be for the time, the rightfulhede of Gods werkyng was shewid to the soule. Rightfulhede hath ii faire properties: it was right and it is full; and so arn al the works of our lord God; and thereto nedith neither the werkyng of mercy ner grace, for it ben al rightfull, wherin feilith nougte. And in another time he shewid for the beholdyng of synne nakidly, as I shal sey, where he usith werkyng of mercy and grace. And this vision was shewid to myne vnderstondeng, for our lord will have the soule turnid truly into the beholdyng of him, and generally of all his werks; for they arn full gode and al his doings be easye and swete, and to gret ease bringing the soule that is turnyd fro the beholdyng of the blind demyng of man onto the faire swete demyng of our lord God; for a man beholdith some dedes wele done and some dedes evil, but our lord beholdyth hem not so; for as al that hath being in kind is of Godds makyng, so is althing that is done in propertie of Gods doing; for it is easye to understonde that the best dede is wele done; and so wele as the best dede is done and the heiest, so wele is the lest dede done; and al in propertie and in the ordir that our lord hath it ordeynit to fro withoute begynning, for ther is no doer but he. I saw ful sekirly that he chongyth never his purpos in no manner thyng, nor never shall, withoute end; for ther was nothyng onknowen to him in his rightfull ordenance from without begynnyng, and therefore altyhyng was sett in ordir, or anything was made, as it should stond withoute end; and no maner thyng shall failen of that poynt; for he made althinge in fulhede of godenes; and therefore the blissid Trinite is ever ful plesid in al his werks. And al this shewid he ful blisfully, meneing thus: 'Se I am

God. Se I am in althing. Se I doe althyng. Se I left never myne hands of myn werks, ne never shall, withoute ende. Se I lede althing to the end I ordeynd it to fro withoute beginnyng be the same might, wisdam and love that I made it. How should anything be amysse?' Thus migtily, wisely and lovinly was the soule examynyd in this vision. Than saw I sothly that me behovyd nedis to assenten with gret reverens, enioyand in God.

12

The iiiith revelation etc., how it likith God rather and better to wash us in his blode from synne than in water, for his blode is most pretious—xii chapter.

And after this I saw, beholding, the body plentiously bleding in seming of the scorgyng, as thus: the faire skynne was brokyn ful depe into the tender flesh with sharpe smyting al about the sweete body; so plenteously the hote blode ran oute that there was neither sene skynne ne wound, but as it were al blode. And whan it come wher it should a fallen downe, than it vanyshid; notwitstondyng, the bleding continued a while til it migt be sene with avisement. And this was so plenteous to my sigt that methowte, if it had be so in kind and in substance for that tyme, it should have made the bed al on blode and a passid over aboute. And than cam to my minde that God hath made waters plentivous in erthe to our service and to our bodily ease, for tender love that he hath to us, but yet lekyth him better that we take full homely[23] [h]is[24] blissid blode to washe us of synne; for there is no licor that is made that he lekyth so wele to give us; for it is most plentivous as it is most pretious, and that be the vertue of his blissid Godhede. And it is our kinde and alblissfully beflowyth us be the vertue of his pretious love. The dereworthy blode of our lord Iesus Criste, as verily as it is most pretious, as verily it is most plentivous. Beholde and se. The pretious plenty of his dereworthy blode descendid downe into helle and braste her

19

bands and deliveryd al that were there which longyd to the curte of hevyn. The pretious plenty of his dereworthy blode overflowith al erth and is redye to wash al creaturs of synne which be of gode will, have ben and shal ben. The pretious plenty of his dereworthy blode ascendid up into hevyn to the blissid body of our lord Iesus Christe, and there is in him bleding and praying for us to the Father—and is and shall be as long as it nedith. And evermore it flowith in all hevyns enioying the salvation of al mankynde that arn there and shal ben, fulfilling the noumber that failith.

13

The vth revelation is that the temptation of the fend is overcome be the passion of Criste, to the encres of ioy of us, and to his peyne, everlestingly—xiii chapter.

And after, or God shewid ony words, he sufferd me to beholden in him a conable tyme, and all that I had sene, and all intellecte that was therein as the simplicite of the soule migte take it. Than he, without voice and openyng of lippis, formys in my soule these words: 'Herewith is the fend overcome.' These words seyd our lord menening his blissid passion as he shewid aforn. In this shewid our lord that the passion of him is the overcomming of the fend. God shewid that the fend hath now the same malice that he had aforn the incarnation; and as sore he travilith and as continually he seeth that all sent[25] of salvation ascappyn him worshipply be the vertue of Cristes pretious passion; and that is his sorow, and ful evyl he is attemyd; for all that God sufferith him to doe turnith into ioy and him to shame and wo; and he hath as mech sorow when God givith him leave to werkyn as when he werkyth not; and that is for he may never doe as yvel as he would, for his migte is al tokyn in Godds hand. But in God may be no wreth, as to my syte, for our gode lord endlesly hath regarde to his owne worshippe and to the profite of al that shall be savid. With might and right he withstondith the

20

reprovid, the which of mallice and shrewidnes bysyen hem to contriven and to done agens Gods wille. Also I saw our lord scorne his malice and nowten his onmigte, and he wil that we doe so. For this sigte I lavhyd migtily, and that made hem to lavhyn that were about me, and ther lavhyng was a likeing to me. I thowte that I wold that al myn evyn christen had ben[26] as I saw, and than should thei al lavhyn with me. But I saw not Criste lawhyn; for I understode that we may lavhyn in comforting of ourselfe and ioying in God, for the devil is overcome. And then[27] I saw him scorne his malice, it was be ledyng of myn understondyng into our lord, that is to sey, an inward sheweing of sothfastnes, withoute chongyng of chere; for, as to my sight, it is a worshipfull property that is in God, which is durabil. And after this I fel into a sadhede and seid: 'I se iii things [g]ame,[28] scorne and arneste. I se [g]ame[29] that the fend is overcome. I se scorne that God scornith him and he shal be scornyd. And I se arneste that he is overcome be the blissfull passion and deth of our lord Iesus Criste that was done in ful arnest and with sad travelle.' And I seid 'He is scornid', I mene that God scornith him: that is to sey, for he seeth him now as he shall done withoute ende; for in this God shewid that the fend is dampnid; and this ment I when I seid 'He shall be scornyd': at domysday generally of all that shal be savyd, to hose consolation he hath gret invye; for than he shall seen that all the wo and tribulation that he hath done to them shal be turnid to encres of their ioy without ende, and al the peyne and tribulation that he would a brought hem to shal endlesly goe with him to helle.

14

The vi revelation is of the worshippfull thanke with which he rewardith his serva[n]ts,[30] and it hath iii ioyes—xiiii chapter.

After this our good lord seid: 'I thanke thee of thy travel and namely of thy youthe.' And in this myn understondyng was lifted up into hevyn where I saw our lord as a lord in his own house, which hath clepid al his derworthy servants and freinds to a solemne feste. Than I saw the lord take no place in his owne house, but I saw him rialy regne in his hous, and fulfillid it with ioy and mirth, hymselfe endlesly to gladen and to solacyn his derworthy frends ful homeley and ful curtesly, with mervelous melody of endles love in his owen faire blissid chere; which glorious chere of the Godhede fulfillith hevyns of ioy and bliss. God shewid iii degrees of blis that every soule shal have in hevyn that wilfully hath servid God in any degre in erthe. The first is the worshipful thanke of our lord God that he shal recevyn whan he is deliverid of peyne; this thanke is so high and so worshipful that him thinkith it fillith him thow there were no more; for methowte that all the peyne and travel that might be suffryd of all liveing men might not deserve the worshipfull thanke that one man shall have that wilfully hath servid God. The iid, that all the blissid creatures that arn in hevyn shall se that worshipfull thankyng, and he makyth his service knowen to al that arn in hevyn. And in this time this example was shewid: a king, if he thanke his servants it is a gret worship to hem, and if he makyth it knowen to all the reme, than is his worshippe mekil incresid. The iii is that as new and as lekyng as it is underfongyn that tyme, rigte so shall it lesten withoute ende. And I saw that homely and swetely was this shewid: that the age of every man shal be knowen in hevyn, and shal be rewardid for his wilful service and for his time; and namely the age of hem that wilfully and frely offer her yongith to God passingly is rewardid and wonderly is thankyd; for I saw that whan or what tyme a man or woman be truly turnid to God, for on day service and for his endles wille, he shall have al these iii degres of blisse. And the more that the lovand soule seeth this curtesy of God, the lever he is to serve him al the dayes of his life.

15

*The viith revelation is of oftentymes felyng of wele and wo etc.,
and how it is expedient that man sumtymes be left withoute
comfort, synne it not causeing—xv chapter.*

And after this he shewid a soveren gostly lekyng in my soule.
I was fulfillid of the everlesting sekirnes migtily susteinid
withoute any peynful drede. This felyng was so gladd and so
gostly that I was in al peace and in reste that there was nothing
in erth that should a grevid me. This lestinid but a while and
I was turnyd and left to myselfe in hevynes and werines of my
life and irkenes of myselfe that onethis I coude have patience
to leve. There was no comfort nor none ease to me but feith,
hope and charite, and these I had in truthe, but litil in feling.
And anone, after this, our blissid lord gave me ageyne the
comfort and the rest in soule, in likyng and sekirnes so blisful
and so mycti that no drede, no sorow, ne peyne bodily that
might be suffrid should have desesid me. And than the peyne
shewid ageyn to my feling, and than the ioy and the lekyng,
and now that one, and now that other, dyvers times—I suppose
aboute xx tymes. And in the same tyme of ioy I migte have
seid with Seynt Paul: 'Nothing shal depart me fro the charite
of Criste'. And in the peyne I migte have seid with Peter:
'Lord, save me, I perish'. This vision was shewid me, after
myn vnderstondyng, that it is spedeful to some soulis to fele
on this wise, somtime to be in comfort, and somtyme to faile
and to be left to hemselfe. God wille we knowen that he kepyth
us even alike sekir in wo and in wele. And for profitt of manys
soule a man is sumtyme left to himselfe, althowe synne is not
ever the cause; for in this tyme I synned not wherfore I shulde
be left to myselfe, for it was so soden. Also I deservyd not to
have this blissid felyng. But frely our lord gevyth whan he
wille, and suffrith us in wo sumtyme. And both is one love;
for it is Godds wil we hold us in comfort with al our migte,
for blisse is lestinge withoute ende, and peyne is passand and

shal be browte to nougte to hem that shall be savyd. And therefore it is not Godds will that we folow the felynge of peyne in sorow and mornyng for hem, but sodenly passing over and holden us in endless likyng.

16

The viiith revelation is of the last petivous peynes of Christe deyeng, and discoloryng of his face and dreyeng of his flesh —xvi chapter.

After this Criste shewid a partie of his passion nere his deyeng. I saw his swete face as it was drye and blodeles with pale deyeng; and sithen more pale, dede, langoring, and than turnid more dede into blew, and sithen more brown blew, as the flesh turnyd more depe dede; for his passion shewid to me most propirly in his blissid face, and namly in his lippis; there I saw these iiii colowres, tho that were aforn freshe, redy and likyng to my sigte. This was a swemful chonge to sene this depe deyeng, and also the nose clange and dryed, to my sigte, and the swete body was brown and blak, al turnyd oute of faire lifely colowr of hymselfe onto drye deyeng; for that eche[31] tyme that our lord and blissid savior deyid upon the rode it was a dry, harre wynde and wond colde, as to my sigte; and what tyme the pretious blode was blede oute of the swete body that migte pass therfro, yet there dwellid a moysture in the swete flesh of Criste, as it was shewyd. Blodeleshede and peyne dryden within and blowyng of wynde and cold commyng fro withouten metten togeder in the swete body of Criste. And these iiii, tweyn withouten, and tweyn within, dryden the fleshe of Criste be process of tyme. And thow this peyne was bitter and sharpe, it was full longe lestyng, as to my sighte, and peynfully dreyden up all the lively spirits of Crists fleshe. Thus I saw the swete fleshe dey, in semyng be party after party, dryande with mervelous peynys. And as longe as any spirit had life in Crists fleshe, so longe sufferid he peyne. This longe pynyng semyd to me as if he had bene

24

seven night ded, deyand, at the poynt of out passing away, sufferand the last peyne. And than I said it semyd to me as if he had bene seven night dede, it menyth that the swete body was so discoloryd, so drye, so clongen, so dedely and so petevous as he had be seven night dede, continuly deyand. And methowte, the deyeng of Crists flesh was the most peyne, and the last, of his passion.

17

Of the grevous bodyly threst of Criste causyd iiii wysys, and of his petovous coronyng, and of the most payne to a kinde lover—xvii[32] chapter.

And in this deyng was browte to my mynde the words of Criste: 'I threst'; for I saw in Criste a doble threst: one bodely, another gostly the which I shal speke of in the xxxi chapter; for this word was shewid for the bodyly threst the which I understode was causid of failyng of moysture, for the blissid flesh and bonys was left al alone without blode and moysture. The blissid bodye dreid alone long tyme, with wryngyng of the naylys and weyte of the bodye; for I understode that for tenderness of the swete hands and of the swete fete, be the gretnes, hardhede and grevoushed of the naylis, the wounds wexid wider and the body saggid for weyte be long tyme hanging; and peircing and wrangyng of the hede and byndyng of the crowne, al bakyn with drye blode, with the swete heire clyngand, and the drye flesh, to the thornys, and the thornys to the flesh deyand; and in the begynnyng, while the flesh was fresh and bledand, the continuant sytyng of the thornys made the wounds wyde. And ferthermore I saw that the swete skyn and the tender flesh, with the heere and the blode, was al rasyd and losyd abov from the bone with the thornys where thowe[33] it were daggyd on many pecys, as a clith that were saggand, as it wold hastely have fallen of for hevy and lose while it had kynde moysture; and that was grete sorow and drede to me, for methowte I wold not for my life a sen it fallen.

How it was don I saw not, but understode it was with the sharpe thornys and the boystrous and grevous setting on of the garland onsparably and without pety. This continuid a while and sone it began to chongyn, and I beheld and merveled how it migt ben. And than I saw it was for it began to dreyen and stynte a party of the weyte and sette abute the garland. And thus it envyronyd al aboute, as it were garland upon garland. The garland of the thornys was dyed with the blode, and the tother garland and the hede, al was on colour, as cloderyd blode whan it is drey. The skynne of the flesh that semyd of the face and of the body was smal, ronkyllid, with a tannyd colour, lyke a dry borde whan it is akynned;[34] and the face more browne than the body. I saw iiii maner of dryengs: the first was blodeless; the secund was payne folowyng after; the thred, hangyng up in the eyr as men hang a cloth to drye; the forth, that the bodily kynd asky[d][35] licour and ther was no maner of comfort mynystid to hym in al his wo and disese. A! herd and grevous was his peyne, but mech more hard and grevous it was whan the moysture faylid and al beganne to drye thus clyngand. These were the paynys that shewdyn in the blissful hede: the first wrought to the deyng whyl it was moyst; and that other, slow, with clyngyng dryand, with blowing of the wynde from withowten that dryed him more, and peynd with cold, that myn herte can [thingke];[36] and other paynys; for which paynys I saw that all is to litil that I can sey, for it may not be told. The which shewing of Cristes peynys fillid me ful of payne, for I wiste wele he suffryd but onys, but, as he wold shewn it me and fillen me with mynde as I had aforn desyryd. And in al this tyme of Cristes paynys I felte no payn but for Cristes paynys. Than thowte me 'I knew but litil what payne it was that I askyd', and as a wretch repentid me, thynkand if I had wiste what it had be, lothe me had be to have praydd it; for methowte it passid bodely dethe, my paynes. I thowte: 'Is any payne like this?' And I was answered in my reason: 'Helle is another payne, for there is despeyr. But of al paynes that leden to salvation, this is the most payne: to se thy love suffir.' How might any payne be more to me than to se him that [is][37] al my life, al my blisse and al my ioy suffren? Here felt I sothfastly that I lovyd Criste so mech above myselfe that there was no payne that might be suffrid leke to that sorow that I had to se him in payne.

18

Of the spiritual martyrdam of our lady and other lovers of Criste, and how al things suffryd [with][38] *hym, goode and ylle—xviii chapter.*

Here I saw a part of the compassion of our lady Seynt Mary, for Christe and she were so onyd in love that the gretnes of his lovyng was cause of the mekylhede of hyr payne; for in thys I saw a substance of kynd love, continyyd be grace, that creatures have to hym; which kynde love was most fulsomely shewyd in his swete moder, and overpassyng, for so mech as she lovid him more than al others, hir panys passyd al others; for ever the heyer, the myghtyer, the sweter that the love be, the mor sorow it is to the lover to se that body in payne that is lovid. And al his disciples and al his trew lovers suffrid panys more than ther owne bodyly deyng; for I am sekir, by myn owne felyng, that the lest of hem lovid hym so far above hemself that it passyth al that I can sey. Here saw I a gret onyng betwyx Christe and us, to myn understondyng; for whan he was in payne, we were in payne. And al cretures that might suffre payne suffrid with him, that is to sey, al cretures that God hathe made to our service. The firmament, the erth faledyn for sorow in hyr kynde in the tyme of Crists deyng; for longith it kyndely to thir properte to know hym for ther God in whome al ther vertue stondyth; whan he faylid, than behovyd it nedis to them for kyndes to faylen with hym as mech as thei myght, for sorow of his penys. And thus thei that were his frends suffryd peyne for love. And generaly, al—that is to sey, thei that knew hym not—suffrid for feylyng of al manner of comfort save the myghty privy kepyng of God. I mene of ii manner of folke, as it may be understode by ii personys: that on was Pilate, that other was Sain Dionyse of

27

France, which was that tyme a paynym; for whan he saw wonderous and mervelous sorowes and dreds that befallen in that tyme, he sayd: 'Either the world is now at an end, or ell he that is maker of kynde suffryth.' Wherfor he did write on an auter: 'This is the auter of onknown God.' God of his godenes that maketh the planets and the elements to werkyn of kynd to the blissid man and the cursid, in that tyme it was withdrawen from bothe; wherfore it was that thei that knew him not were in sorow that tyme. Thus was our lord Iesus nawted for us, and we stond al in this manner nowtid with hym; and shal done til we come to his blisse, as I shal sey after.

19

Of the comfortable beholdyng of the crucifyx, and how the desyre of the flesh without consent of the soule is no synne, and the flesh must be in peyne, suffring, til bothe be onyd to Criste—xix chapter.

In this I wold a lokyd up of the crosse, and I durst not, for I weste wele whyl I beheld in the cross I was seker and save; therefore I wold not assenten to put my soule in perel, for beside the crosse was no sekernes for vggyng of fends. Than had I a profir in my reason as it had be frendly seyd to me: 'Loke up to hevyn to his Fader.' And than saw I wele with the feyth that I felte that ther was nothyn betwix the crosse and hevyn that myght have desesyd me. Either me behovyd to loke up, or else to answeren. I answered inwardly with al the myghts of my soule and said: 'Nay, I may not, for thou art my hevyn'. This I seyd for I wold not; for I had lever a ben in that peyne til domysday than to come to hevyn otherwyse than by hym; for I wiste wele that he that bonde me so sore, he sholde onbynde me whan that he wolde. Thus was I lerid to chose Iesus to my hevyn, whome I saw only in payne at that tyme. Me lekyd no other hevyn than Iesus, which shal be my blisse whan I come there. And this hath ever be a comfort to me, that I chose Iesus to my hevyn, be his grace, in al this tyme of passion and sorow. And that hat be a lernyng to me that I should evermor done so, chesyn only Iesus to my hevyn in wele and wo. And thow I as a wretch had repentid me—I sayd aforn if I had wiste what peyne it had be me had be loth to have prayed—here saw I sothly that it was grutching and daming of the flesh without assent of the soule, in whych God assignyth no blame. Repenting and wilful choys be two contrarys which I felte both in one at that tyme; and tho be two parties: that one outward, that other inward. The outeward party is our dedely fleshede which is now in peyne and wo, and shal be in this life, whereof I felt mech in this tyme, and that party was that repented. The inward party is an high, blissfull life which is al in pece and in love, and this was more privily felte; and this party is in which mightyly, wysly and wilfully I chase Iesus to my hevyn. And in this I saw sothly that the inward party is master and soverayn to the outeward, and not charging ne takyng hede to the will of that, but al the entent and will is sett endlesly to be onyd into our lord Iesus. That the outeward part should draw the inward to assent was not shewid to me; but that the inward drawith the outeward by grace, and bothe shal be onyd in blisse without end by the vertue of Criste: this was shewid.

20

Of the onspekabyl passion of Criste, and of iii things of the passion alway to be remembrid—xx chapter.

And thus I saw our lord Iesus langring long tyme; for the onyng of the Godhede gave strength to the manhode for love to suffre more than al man myght suffryn. I mene not allonly more peyne than al men myght suffre, but also that he suffrid more peyne than al men of salvation that ever was from the first begynnyng into the last day myght tellyn or ful thynkyn, havyng regard to the worthynes of the heyest, worshipful kyng and the shamly, dispitous, peynful dethe; for he that is heyest

29

and worthyest was fullyest nowtyd and utterlyest dispisid; for the hyest poynte that may be sean in the passion is to thynkyn and knowen what he is that suffryd.[39] And in this he browte a part in mende the heyte and noblyth of the glorias Godhede, and therwith the pretioushed and the tendernes of the blisfull body, which be together onyd, and also the lothhede that is in our kynd to suffre peyne; for as mech as he was most tender and clene, ryght so he was most strong and myghty to suffir; and for every manny synne that shall be savid he suffrid; and every manys sorow and desolation he saw and sorowid for kyndenes and love; for in as mekyl as our lady sorowid for his peynes, as mekyl he suffrid sorrow for her sorow, and more, in as mekyl as the swete manhode of hym was worthier in kynd. For as long as he was passible he suffryd for us and sorowyd for us; and now he is uprysyn and no more passibyl, yet he suffryt with us. And I, beholdyng al this be his grace, saw that the love of hym was so strong whych he hath to our soule that wilfully he ches it with gret desyr and myldly he suffrid it with wel payeyng; for the soule that beholdyth it thus, when it is touchid be grace, he shal veryly se that the peynys of Crists passion passen al peynys: that is to sey, which peynys shal be turnyd into everlestyng passyng ioyes by the vertue of Crists passion.

21

Of iii beholdyngs in the passion of Criste, and how we be now deyng in the crosse with Criste, but his chere puttyt away al peyne—xxi chapter.

Tis Goddys wille, as to myn vnderstondyng, that we have iii manner of beholdyngs in his blissid passion. The first is the herd peyn that he suffrid, with contrition and compassion; and that shewid our lord in this tyme and gave me myght and grace to se it. And I loked after the departing with al my myght and [wende][40] have seen the body al ded, but I saw hym not so. And ryth in the same tyme that methowte, be semyng, the life

30

myght ne lenger lesten and the shewyng of the end behovyd nedis to be,[41] sodenly, I beholdyng in the same crosse, he chongyd his blissfull chere. The chongyng of his blisful chere chongyd myn, and I was as glad and mery as it was possible. Than browte our lord merily to my mynde: 'Where is now ony poynte of the peyne or of thin agreefe?' And I was full merry. I understode that we be now, in our lords menyng, in his crosse with hym in our peynys and our passion, deyng; and we wilfully abydyng in the same cross with his helpe and his grace into the last poynte, sodenly he shall chonge his chere to us, and we shal be with hym in hevyn. Betwix that one and that other shal be no tyme, and than shal al be browte to ioy; and so mente he in this shewyng: 'Where is now ony poynt of thy peyne or thyn agreefe?' And we shal be full blissid. And here saw I sothfastly that if he shewid now us his blissful chere ther is no peyne in erth, nor in other place, that should us agrevyn, but al things should be to us ioy and blisse. But for he shewith to us time of passion as he bare in this life and his crosse, therefore we arn in desese and travel with hym as our frelete askyth. And the cause why he suffrith is for he wil of his godeness make us the heyer with hym in his bliss; and for this litil peyne that we suffre here we shal have an hey, endles knowyng in God, whych we myght never have without that. And the harder our peynys have ben with him in his cross, the more shall our worshippe be with hym in his kyngdom.

22

[T]he[42] ix revelation is o[ff][43] the lekyng etc., of iii hevyns and the infinite love of Criste desiring everday to suffre for us if he myght, althow it is not nedeful—xxii chapter.

Than [seide][44] our good lord Iesus Christe, askyng: 'Art thou wele payd that I suffrid for thee?' I sayd: 'Ya good lord, gramercy. Ya good lord, blissid mot thou be!' Than seyd Iesus, our kinde lord: 'If thou art payde, I am payde. It is a ioy, a blis, an endles lekyng to me that ever suffrid I passion for the; and if I myht suffre more, I wold suffre more.' In this felyng my vnderstondyng was lifte up into hevyn, and there I saw thre hevyns, of which syght I was gretly mervelyd. And thow[45] I se thre hevyns, and all in the blissid manhode of Criste, non is more, non is less, non is heyer, non is lower, but evyn lyke in blis. For the first hevyn Christe shewyd me his Fader, in no [b]odyly[46] lyknes, but in his properte and in his werkyng: that is to sey, I saw in Criste that the Fader is. The werkyng of the Fader is this: that he gevyth mede to his Son, Iesus Criste. This geft and this mede is so blisful to Iesus that his Fader myht have goven hym no mede that myght have lykyd hym better. The first hevyn, that is the plesyng of the Fader, shewid to me as an hevyn, and it was ful blisfull, for he is ful plesed with al the dedes that Iesus hath done aboute our salvation; wherefore we be not only his be his beying, but also by the curtes geft of his Fader we be his blis, we be his mede, we be his worshippe, we be his corone—and this was a singular mervel and a full delectable beholdyng, that we be his corone. This that I sey is so grete blis to Iesus that he settith at nowte al his travel and his herd passion and his cruel and shamful deth. And in these words, 'If that I might suffre more, I would suffer more', I saw sothly that as often as he myght deyen, so often he wold, and love should neve[r][47] let him have rest til he had don it. And I beheld with gret diligens for to wetyn how often he would deyn if he myght, and sotly the noumbre passid myn understondyng and my wittis so fer that my reson myghte not, ne coude, comprehend it. And whan he had thus oft deyid, or should, yet he would set it at nowte for love; for al thynkyth him but litil in reward of his love; for thowe the swete manhood of Criste might suffre but onys, the godenes in him may never sesin of profir; everyday he is redy to the same if it myght be; for if he seyd he wold for my love make new hevyns and new erth, it were but litil in reward, for this might be done everyday if he wold, withoute any travel; but for to dey for my love so often that the noumbre passith creature reson, it is the heyest profir that our lord God myght make to manys soule, as to my syte. Than menyth he thiss:

'How shold it than be that I shold not do for thi love al that I myght—which dede grevyth me not sith I wold for thi love dey so often having no reward to my herd peynys—?' And here saw I for the second beholdyng in this blissid passion the love that made him to suffre passith as far al his peynes as hevyn is above erth; for the peynes was a nobele, worshipfull dede don in a tyme be the werkyng of love; and love was without begynnyng, is, and shall be without endyng; for which love he seyd ful swetely these words: 'If I myght suffre more, I wold suffre more. He seyd not 'If it were nedeful to suffre more', for thow it were not nedeful, if he myght suffre more, he wold. This dede and this werke about our salvation was ordeynyd as wele as God myght ordeyn it. And here I saw a full blisse in Criste; for his blisse shold not a be full if it myte any better have be done.

23

How Criste wil we ioyen with hym gretly in our redemption and to desire grace of hym that we may so doe—xxiii chapter.

And in these iii words 'It is a ioy, a blis, an endles lykyng to me' were shewid iii hevyns, as thus: for the ioy I vnderstode the plesance of the Fader; and for the blis, the worshippe of the Son; and for the endles lykyng, the Holy Gost. The Fader is plesid, the Son is worshippid, the Holy Gost lykith. And here saw I for the thred beholdyng in his blisful passion: that is to sey, the ioy and the blis that make hym to lekyn it; for our curtes lord shewid his passion to me in v manners: of which the first is the bledyng of the hede, the iid is discoloryng of his face, the iiid is the plentivous bledyng of the body in semys of the scorgyng, the iiiith is the depe deyng—these iiii are aforseyd for the peynys of the passion—and the vth is that was shewid for the ioy and the bliss of the passion; for it is Goddys wille that we have trew lekyng with hym in our salvation, and therin he wil we be myghtyly comfortid and strengthnid, and thus wil he merily with his grace that our soule be occupyed; for we arn his blisse; for in us he lekyth without end and so shal we in hym with his grace. And al that he hath done for us, and doth, and ever shal, was never coste ne charge to hym, ne myte be; but only that he dede in our manhood, begynnyng at the sweete incarnation and lesting to the blissid upriste on Esterne morow, so long durid the cost and the charge aboute our redemption in dede, of which dede he enioyeth endlesly, as it is afornseyd. Iesus wil we takyn hede to the blis that is in the blisful Trinite of our salvation and that we desiren to have as mech gostly lykyng, with his grace, as it is afornseyd: that is to sey, that the likyng of our salvation be like to the ioy that Criste hath of our salvation as it may be whil we arn here. Al the Trinite wroute in the passion of Criste, minystryng abundance of vertues and plenty of grace to us be hym, but only the mayden son suffrid; whereof all the blissid Trinite endlesly enioyeth. A[n]d[48] this was shewid in these words: 'Art thou wel payd?' and be that other word that Criste sayd, 'If thou art payed, than am I paide', as if he sayd: 'It is ioy and likyng enow to me, and I aske nowte ell of the for my travel but that I myght wel payen the.' And in this he browte to mend the property of a glad gevere: a glad gever takyth but litil hede of the thyng that he gevith, but al his desire and al his intent is to plesyn hym and solacyn hym to whome he gevyth it; and if the receiver take the geft heyly and thankfully, than the curtes gever settith at nowte all his coste and al his travel for ioy and delite that he hath for he hath plesid and solacid hym that he lovyth. Plenteously and fully was this shewid. Thynke also wisely of the gretnes of this word 'ever'; for in that was shewid an high knowing of love that he hath in our salvation, with manyfold ioyes that folow of the passion of Criste; one is that he ioyeth that he hath don it in dede, and he shal no more suffre; another, that he browte us up into hevyn and made us for to be his corone and endles blisse; another is that he hath therwith bawte us from endless peynys of helle.

24

Than with a glad chere our lord loked into his syde and beheld, enioyand; and with his swete lokyng he led forth the understondyng of his creture be the same wound into his syde withinne. And than he shewid a faire delectabil place, and large enow for al mankynd that shal be save to resten in pece and in love. And therwith he browte to mende his dereworthy blode and pretious water which he lete poure al oute for love. And with the swete beholdyng he shewid his blisful herte even cloven on two. And with this swete enioyyng he shewid onto myn vnderstondyng, in party, the blissid Godhede, steryng than the pure soule for to vnderstonde, as it may be said, that is to mene, the endles love that was with- out begynnyng, and is, and shal be ever. And with this our gode lord seyd ful blisfully 'Lo how that I lovid the', as if he had seid: 'My derling, behold and se thy lord, thy God, that is thy maker and thyn endles ioy. Se what likyng and bliss I have in thy salvation, and for my love enioy now with me.' And also for more vnderstondyng this blissid word was seyd: 'Lo how I lovid the. Behold and se that I lovid the so mekyl ere I deyd for the that I wold dey for the; and now I hay deyd for the, and suffrid wilfuly that I may. And now is al my bitter peyne and al my hard travel turnyd to endles ioy and bliss to me and to the. How should it now be that thou should onything pray me that lekyth me, but if I shuld ful gladly grant it the? For my lekyng is thy holynes and thyn endles ioy and bliss with me.' This is the understondyng simply as I can sey of this blissid word: 'Lo how I lovid the.' This shewid our gode lord for to make us glad and mery.

25

The xi revelation is an hey gostly shewing of his moder—xxv chapter.

And with this same chere of myrth and ioy our gode lord lokyd downe on the ryte syde and browte to my mynde where our lady stode in the tyme of his passion; and seid 'Wilt the se her?' and in this swete word, as if he had seyd: 'I wote wele thou wold se my blissid moder, for after myselfe she is the heyest ioy that I myte shew the, and most lykyng and worshippe to me; and most she is desyrid to be seene of my blissid cretures.' And for the hey, mervelous, singular love that he hath to this swete mayden, his blissid moder, our lady Seyt Mary, he shewid hir heyly enioyng, as be the menyng of these swete words, as if he seyd: 'Wil thou se how I love hir, that thou myte ioy with me in the love that I have in her and she in me?' And also to more vnderstondyng this swete word our lord God spekyth to al mankynde that shal be save as it were al to one person, as if he seyd: 'Wilt thou seen in hir how thou art lovid? For thy love I made her so hey, so noble and so worthy; and this likyth me, and so wil I that it doith the.' For after hymselfe she is the most blisful syte. But herof am I not lerid to longen to seen hir bodyly presense while I am here, but the vertues of hir blissid soule: her truth, her wisdam, hir charite; wherby I may leryn to know myselfe and reverently drede my God. And whan our gode lord had shewid this and seid this word, 'Wilt thou seen hir?' I answerid and seyd: 'Ya good lord, gramercy. Ya good lord, if it be thy wille.' Oftentymes I prayd this and I wend a seen hir in bodily presens, but I saw hir not so. And Iesus in that word shewid me a gostly sigte of hir; ryte as I had seen hir aforn litil and simple, so he shewid hir than hey and noble and glorious and plesyng to hym above al creatures. And he wil that it be knowen that al those that lyke in hym should lyken in hir and in the lykyng that he hath in hir and she in him. And to more

36

understondyng he shewid this example: as, if a man love a creature syngularly above al creatures, he wil make al creature to loven and to lyken that creature that he lovith so mekyl. And in this word that Iesus seid, 'Wilt thou se hir?' methowte it was the most likyng word that he might have gove me of hir with the gostly shewyng that he gave me of hir; for our lord shewid me nothyng in special but our lady Seynt Mary; and hir he shewid iii tymys: the first was as she grevid,[50] the iid was as she was in hir sorows under the cross, the iii is as she is now in likyng, worshippe and ioye.

26

The xii revelation is that the lord our God is al sovereyn beyng—xxvi chapter.

And after this our [lorde][51] shewid hym more gloryfyed, as to my syte, than I saw him beforne, wherin I was lernyd that our soule shal never have rest til it comith to hym knowing that he is fulhede of ioy, homely and curtesly blisful and very life. Our lord Iesus oftentymes seyd: 'I it am, I it am; I it am that is heyest; I it am that thou lovist; I it am that thou lykyst; I it am that thou servist; I it am that thou longyst; I it am that thou desyrist; I it am that thou menyst; I it am that is al; I it am that holy church prechyth and teachyth the; I it am that shewed me here to thee.' The nombre of the words passyth my witte and al my vnderstondyng and al my mights, and it arn the heyest, as to my syte; for therin is comprehendid—I cannot tellyn; but the ioy that I saw in the shewyng of them passyth al that herte may willen and soule may desire; and therefore the words be not declaryd here but every man after the grace that God gevyth him in vnderstondyng and lovyng receive hem in our lords menyng.

27

The xiiith revelation is that our lord God wil that we have grete regard to all his deds that he hav don in the gret noblyth of al things makyng and of etc., how synne is not knowin but by the peyn—xxvii[52] chapter.

After this the lord browte to my mynd the longyng that I had to hym aforn; and I saw that nothyng letted me but synne, and so I beheld generally in us al. And methowte if synne had not a ben, we should al a ben clene and like to our lord as he made us; and thus, in my foly, aforn this tyme often I wondrid whi by the gret forseyng wysdam of God the begynnyng of synne was not lettid; for than, thowte me, al shuld a be wele. This steryng was mikel to forsakyn, and nevertheless mornyng and sorow I made therefor without reason and discretion. But Iesus, that in this vision enformid me of all that me neydyth, answerid by this worde and seyd: 'Synne is behovabil, but al shal be wel, and al shal be wel, and al manner of thyng shal be wele.' In this nakid word 'synne' our lord browte to my mynd generally al that is not good, and the shamfull dispite and the utter nowtyng that he bare for us in this life, and his dyeng, and al the peynys and passions of al his creatures, gostly and bodyly—for we be all in party nowtid, and we shall be nowtid followyng our master Iesus till we be full purgyd: that is to sey, till we be fully nowtid of our dedly flesh and of al our inward affections which arn not very good—, and the beholdyng of this, with al peynys that ever wern or ever shal be; and with al these I understond the passion of Criste for most peyne and overpassyng. And al this was shewid in a touch and redily passid over into comforte; for our good lord wold not that the soule were afferd of this uggly sigte. But I saw not synne; for I beleve it hath no maner of substance ne party of being, ne it myght not be knowin but by the peyne that it is cause of; and thus peyne, it is somethyng, as to my syte, for a tyme, for it purgith and makyth us to knowen ourselfe and askyn mercy; for the passion of our lord is comforte to us agens al this, and so is his blissid wille. And for the tender love that our good lord hath to all that shal be save he comfortith redyly and swetely, menyng thus: 'It is sothe that synne is cause of all this peyne, but al shal be wele, and al shall be wele, and all manner thing shal be wele.' These words were seyd full tenderly, shewyng no manner of blame to me ne to non that shall be safe. Than were it a gret unkindness to blame or wonder on God for my synne, seith[53] he blamyth not me for synne. And in these same words I saw a mervelous hey privitye hid in God, which privity he shall openly make knowen to us in hevyn; in which knowyng we shal verily see the cause why he suffrid synne to come; in which syte we shall endlesly ioyen in our lord God.

28

How the children of salvation shal be shakyn in sorowis, but Criste enioyth wyth compassion; and a remedye agayn tribulation—xxviiith chapter.

Thus I saw how Criste hath compassion on us for the cause of synne. And ryte as I was aforn in the passion of Criste fulfillid with peyne and compassion, like in this I was fulfilld a party with compassion of al myn even Cristen; for that wel, wel belovid people that shal be savid; that is to sey, Gods servants, holy church, shal be shakyn in sorows and anguis and tribulation in this world as men shakyn a cloth in the wynde. And as to this our lord answerid in this manner: 'A gret thing shall I makyn hereof in hevyn, of endles worshipps and everlestyng ioyes.' Ya, so ferforth I saw that our lord ioyth of the tribulations of his servants with reuth and compassion, to ech person that he lovyth to his bliss for to bringen, he levyth upon them something that is no lak in hys syte, wherby thei are lakid and dispisyd in thys world, scornyd, rapyd and outcasten; and this he doith for to lettyn the harme that thei shuld take of the pompe and the veyn glory of this wrechid lif, and mak ther way redy to come to hevyn, and heynen them in his bliss without end lestyng; for he seith: 'I shall al tobreke you for your veyn affections and your vicious pryde; and after that I shal togeder gader you and make you mylde and meke, clene and holy, by onyng to me.' And than I saw that ech kynde compassion that man hath on his even cristen with charite, it is Criste in him. That same nowthyng that was shewid in his passion, it was shewid ageyn here in this compassion wherein were ii maner of vnderstondyngs in our lords menyng: the one was the bliss that we arn bowte to wherin he will be enioyen; that other is for comforte in our peyne; for he will that we wettyn that it shal al be turnyd to worshippe and profite be vertue of his passion, and that we wetyn that we suffir not alone but with him, and seen hym our grounde, and that we seen his penys and his nowtyng passith so fer al that we may sufre that it may not be ful thowte. And the beholdyng of this will save us from gruching and dispeir in the felyng of our peynys; and if we se sothly that our synne deservyth it, yet his love excusith us, and of his gret curtesye he doith awey al our blame, and he holdyth us with ruth and pite as childer, inocentes and vnlothfull.

29

Adam synne was gretest, but the satisfaction for it is more plesyng to God than ever was the synne harmfull—xxix chapter.

But in this I stode beholdyng generally, swemly and mournyng, seyng thus to our lord in my menyng with ful grete drede: 'A! good lord, how myte al ben wele for the grete hurte that is come by synne to the creatures?' And here I desirid, as I durst, to have sum more open declaryng wherwith I myte be esyd in this. And to this our blisfull lord answerd full mekely, and with ful lovely chere, and shewid that Adams synne was the most harme that ever was don, or ever shal, to the world ende; and also he shewid that this is openly knowen in al holy church in erth. Furthermore he leryd that I should behold the glorious asyeth; for this asyeth making is more plesyng to God and more worshipfull for manys salvation, without comparison, than ever was the synne of Adam harmfull. Than menyth our blissid lord thus in this techyng, that we should take hede to this: 'For sythe I have made wele the most harme, than it is my wil that thou knowe thereby that I shal make wel al that less.'

30

How we shuld ioye and trusten in our saviour Iesus, not presumyng to know his privy counsell—xxx chapter.

He gave me understondyng of ii parties. That one party is our savior and our salvation; this blissid parte is hopyn and clere and faire and lite and plentivous, for al manky[n]d[54] that is of good wille and shal be is comprehendid in this parte; herto arn we bounden of God and drawen and coun[c]ellid[55] and lerid inwardly be the Holy Gost and outwardly be holy church in the same grace; in this will our lord we be occupyed, ioyeng in him for he onioyeth in us; and the more plentivously that we take of this with reverens and mekenes, the more thanke we deserven of hym and the more spede to ourselfe; and thus, may we sey, enioyeng our part is our lord. That other is hid and sperid from us: that is to sey, al that is besiden our salvation; for it is our lords privy councell, and it longyth to the ryal lordship of God to have his privy councell in pece, and it longyth to his servant, for obedience and reverens, not to wel wetyn his conselye. Our lord hath pety and compassion on us for that sum creatures make them so besy therin; and I am sekir if we wisten how mekil we shuld plese hym and ese ourselfe to leven it, we wolden. The seynts that be in hevyn, thei wil nothyng wetyn but that our lord will shewen hem, and also their charite and their desire is rulid after the wil of our lord; and thus owen we to willen like to hem: than shal we nothyng willen ne desiren but the wille of our lord like as thei do; for we arn al on in Goddis menyng. And here was I lernyd

that we shal trosten and enioyen only in our savior blisful
Iesus for althynge.

31

Off the longyng and the spiritual threst of Criste, which lestyth
and shall lesten til domysday; and be the reason of his body he
is not yet full gloryfyed ne al unpassible—xxxi chapter.

And thus our good lord answerid to al the question and doubts
that I myte makyn, sayeing ful comfortably: 'I may makyn
althing wele; I can make althing wele and I wil make althyng
wele and I shall make althyng wele; and thou shal se thiself
that al manner of thyng shal be wele.' That he seyth 'I may',
I understond for the Fader; and he seith 'I can', I understond
for the Son; and where he seith 'I will', I understond for the
Holy Gost; and wher he seith 'I shall', I understond for the
unite of the blissid Trinite, iii persons and one trouthe; and
where he seith 'Thou shal se thiselfe', I understond the onyng
of al mankynd that [shalle][56] be save into the blisful Trinite.
And in thes v words God wil be onclosid in rest and pece; and
thus shal the gostly threst of Criste have an end; for this is the
gostly thrist of Criste: the luflongyng that lestith and ever shal,
til we se that syte on domysday. For we that shal be save, and
shal be Crists ioye and his blis, some be yet here, and some
be to cum; and so shal sum be in to that day. Therefore this
is his thirst: a love longyng to have us al togeder hole in him
to his blis, as to my syte; for we be not now as f[u]lly[57] hole
in him as we shal be then. For we knowen in our feith, and
also it was shewid in alle, that Criste Iesus is both God and
man. And arnernst the Godhede, he is hymselfe heyest blis,
and was from without begynnyng and shall be from withoute
end; which endles blis may never be heyned ne lownyd in the
selfe; for this was plentiously sen in every shewyng and
namely in the twelfth wher he seith: 'I am that is heyest.' And
anernst Crists manhood, it is knowen in our feith, and also
shewyd, that he, with the vertue of Godhede, for love to bring

42

us to his blis, suffrid peynys and passions, and deid; and these be the werks of Crists manhode wherin he enioyeth, and that shewid he in the ix revelation wher he seith: 'It is a ioye, a blis, an endles lykyng to me that ever I suffrid passion for the.' And this is the blis of Crists werks and thus he menyth where he seith in the selfe shewing: we be his blis, we be his mede, we be his worship, we be his corone. For anernst that Criste is our hede, he is glorifyed and onpassible, and anernst his body in which al his members be knitt, he is not yet ful gloryfyed ne al onpassible; for the same desire and threst that he had upon the cross, which desire, longyng and thrist, as to my syte, was in him fro withoute begynnyng, the same hath he yet, and shal into the tyme that the last soule that shal be savid is cum up to his bliss; for as verily as there is a properte in God of ruth and pity, as veryly there is a property in God of threst and longyng. And of the vertue of this longyng in Criste we have to longen ageyn to him, withoute which no soule comyth to hevyn. And this propertye of longyng and threst comyth of the endles goodnes of God, ryte as the property of pite comith of his endles goodnes, and thow longyng and pite arn two sundry properties, as to my syte; and in this stondyth the poynt of the gostly thrist, which is lestyng in hym as long as we be in nede, us drawing up to his blis; and al this was sen in the shewyng of compassion, for that shal secyn on domysday. Thus he hath ruth and compassion on us, and he hath longyng to have us, but his wisdam and his love suffrith not the end to cum til the best tyme.

32

How althyng shal be wele and scripture fulfillid, and we must stedfastly holdyn us in the faith of holy chirch, as is Crists wille—xxxii chapter.

On tyme our good lord seid: 'Althyng shal be wele'; and another tyme he seid: 'Thou shalt sen thiself that al manner thyng shal be wele'; and in these ii the soule toke sundry

43

vnderstondyng. On was this: that he wil we wetyn that not only he takith hede to noble thyngs and to grete, but also to litil and to smale, to low and to simple, to on and to other; and so menyth he in that he seith 'Al manner thyngs shal be wele'; for he will we wetyn the leste thyng shal not be forgotten. Another vnderstondyng is this: that there be dedes evyl done in our syte and so grete harm[es][58] takyn that it semyth to us that it were impossibil that ever it shuld cum to gode end; and upon this we loke, sorowyng and morning therefore, so that we cannot restyn us in the blisful beholdyng of God as we shuld doe; and the cause is this: that the use of our reason is now so blynd, so low and so symple that we cannot know that hey, mervelous wisdam, the myte and the goodness of the blisful Trinite; and thus menyth he wher he seith 'Thou shalt se thiself that al maner thyng shal be wele', as if he seid: 'Take now hede faithfully and trostily, and at the last end thou shalt verily sen it in fulhede of ioye.' And thus in these same v wordis afornseid: 'I may make al thyngs wele etc.', I vnderstond a myty comforte of al the works of our lord God that arn for to comen. Ther is a dede the which the blisful Trinite shal don in the last day, as to my syte, and whan the dede shall be, and how it shal be done, it is onknown of all creatures that are beneath Criste, and shal be till whan it is don.[59] And the cause he wil we know is for he wil we be the more esyd in our soule and pesid in love, levyng the beholdyng of al tempests that myte lettyn us of trewth, enioyeng in him. This is the grete dede ordeynyd of our lord God from without begynnyng, treasured and hid in his blissid breast, only knowen to hymself, be which dede he shal make al thyngs wele; for like as the blisful Trinite made al thyngs of nowte, ryte so the same blissid Trinite shal make wele al that is not wele. And in this syte I mervelid gretely and beheld our feith, merveland thus: our feith is g[r]owndid[60] in Goddys word, and it longyth to our feith that we levyn that Goddys word shal be savid in al things; and one peynt of our feith is that many creatures shal be dampyd—as angells that fellyn out of hevyn for pride, which be now fends; and man in herth that deyth oute of the feith of holy church, that is to say, thei that be

44

ethen men and also man that hath receyvid christendam and
livith uncristen life and so deyth out of charite—all these shall
be dampnyd to hel without end, as holy church techyth me to
belevyn. And stondyng al this, methowte it was impossibil that
al manner thyng should be wele as our lord shewid in this
tyme; and as to this I had no other answere in shewyng of our
lord God but this: 'That is impossible to the is not impossible
to me. I shal save my worde in al things and I shal make
althing wele.' Thus I was tawte by the grace of God that I
should stedfastly hold me in the faith as I had afornehand
vnderstonden, and therewith that I should sadly levyn that
althyng shal be wele as our lord shewid in the same tyme; for
this is the great dede that our lord shal done, in which dede
he shal save his word in althing and he shal make wele al that
is not wele. And how it shal be don, there is no creature
benethe Criste that wot it ne shal wetyn it till it is don, as to
the vnderstondyng that I toke of our lords menyng in this
tyme.

33

Al dampnyd soule be dispisid in the syte of God as the devil;
and these revelations withdraw not the feith of holy church, but
comfortith; and the more we besy to know Gods privites the
less we knowen—xxxiii chapter.

And yet in this I desired, as I durst, that I myte have had ful
syte of helle and purgatory. But it was not my mening to
maken privy[61] of anythyng that longyth to the feith—for I
levyd sothfastly that hel and purgatory is for the same end
that holy church techith—but my menyng was that I myte have
seen for leryng in althyng that longyth to my feith wherby I
myte liven the more to Gods worship and to my profit. And
for my desire I coude of this ryte nowte, but as it is aforseid
in the v shewing wher that I saw that the devil is reprovid of
God and endlesly dampned; in which syte I understode that
al creatures that arn of the devils condition in this life and

45

therin enden, there is no more mention made of hem aforn
God and al his holy than of the devil, notwithstondyng that
thei be of mankynd, whether they have be cristenyd or not.
For thow the revelation was made of goodnes, in which was
made litil mention of evil, yet I was not drawne therby from
any poynt of the feith that holy church techyth me to levyn;
for I had syte of the passion of Criste in dyvers shewyngs—in
the first, in the iid, in the v and in the viii—as it is seid aforn,
wheras I had in party a felyng of the sorow of our lady and
of his trew frends that sen hym in peyne, but I saw not so
propirly specyfyed the Iewes that deden hym to ded; notwith-
stondyn, I knew in my feith that thei wer accursid and
dampny(d)[62] without end, savyng those that converten be
grace. And I was strengthyd and lered generaly to kepe me
in the feith in every pointe, and in al as I had afore
vnderstoden, hopyng that I was therin with the mercy and the
grace of God, desyring and prayng in my menyng that I myte
continue therin onto my lifs end. And it is Gods will that we
have gret regard to al his dedes that he hath don,[63] but
evermore it us nedyth levyn the beholdyng what the dede shal
be. And desir we to be leke our brethren which be seynts in
hevyn that wille ryth nowte but God wille, than shal we only
enioyen in God and ben wel payd both with hyding and with
shewyng; for I saw sothly in our lordis menyng: the more we
besyn us to knowen his privities in this or any other thyng,
the ferther shal we be from the knowing therof.

34

God shewyth the privityes necessarye to his lovers, and how
they plese God mekyl that receive diligently the prechyng of
holy church—xxxiiii chapter.

Our lord God shewid to manner of privityes: on is this gret
privyte with al the prive peynts that longen therto, and these
privites he wil we knowen hid into the tyme that he wil clerly
shewen hem to us; that other arn the privytes that he wil

46

maken opyn and knowen to us; for he wil we wetyn that it is
his wil we knowen hem. It arn privytes to us not only that he
wil it ben privytes to us, but it arn privytes to us for our
blyndnes and our onknowyng; and therof hath he gret ruthe,
and therfore he wil hymself maken hem more opyn to us
wherby [w]e [m]ay[64] knowen hym and loven hym and clevyn
to him; for al that is spedeful to us to wetyn and to knowen,
ful curtesly our lord will shewen us[65]—and that is this—with
al the prechyng and techyng of holy church. God shewid ful
gret plesance that he hath in al men and women that mytyly
and mekely and wilfully taken the prechyng and techyng of
holy church; for it is his holy church; he is the ground, he is
the substance, he is the techyng, he is the techer, he is the
leryd,[66] he is the mede wherfor every kynd soule travellith;
and this is knowen and shall be knowen to every soule to
which the Holy Gost declarith it. And hope[67] sothly that al
those that seke this he shal spedyn, for they seky God. Al this
that I have now seid, and more that I shall sey after, is
comfortyng ageyn synne; for in the thred shewyng when I saw
that God doith al that is don, I saw no synne, and than saw I
that al is wele. But whan God shewid me for synne, than seid
he: 'Al shal be wele.'

35

*How God doith al that is good, and suffrith worshipfully al by
his mercy, the which shal secyn whan synne is no longer
suffrid—xxxv chapter.*

And whan God almyty had shewid so plentevously and so
fully of h[y]s[68] godenes, I desired to wetyn[69] a certeyn creature
that I lovid if it shuld continu in good lyvyng, which I hopid
be the grace of God was begonne. And in this syngular desire
it semyd that I lettyd myselfe, for I was not taught in this tyme.
And than was I answerid in my reson, as it were be a freindful
mene: 'Take it generally, and behold the curtesy of the lord
God as he shewith to the; for it is mor worship to God to

47

behold hym in al than in any special thyng.' I asentid and therewith I leryd that it is more worship to God to knowen al things in general than to lyken in onythyng in special. And if I shuld do wysely after this techyng I shuld not only be glad for nothyng in special, ne gretly disesid for no manner of thyng, for 'Al shal be wele'; for the fulhede of ioy is to beholden God in al; for be the same blissid myte, wisdam and love that he made althyng, to the same end our good lord ledyth it continually, and therto hymse[l]fe[70] shal bryng it; and whan it is tyme we shal sen it. And the grounde of this was shewid in the first, and more openly in the iii wher it seyth, 'I saw God in a peynte'. Al that our lord doeth is rythful, and that he suffrith is worshipful; and in these ii is comprehendid good and ille; for al that is good our lord doith, and that is evil our lord suffrrith. I sey not that ony evil is worshipful, but I sey the sufferance of our lord God is worshipfull, wherby his goodnes shal be know withoute end in his mervelous mekeness and myldehede, by the werkyng of mercy and grace. Rythfulhede is that thyng that is so goode that may not be better than it is; for God hymselfe is very rythfulhede and al his werkes arn don rythfully as they arn ordeynid from without begynnyng [by][71] his hey myte, his hey wisdom, his hey goodnes. And ryth as he ordeyned onto the best, ryth so he werkyth continualy and ledyth it to the same end; and he is ever ful plesid with hymse[l]f[72] and with al his werks. And the beholdyng of this blisful accord is ful swete to the soule [that][73] seith by grace. Al the sowlys that shal be savid in hevyn withoute ende be mad rythful in the syte of God, and be his owen goodnes; in which rythfulhede we arn endlesly kept and mervelously, aboven al creatures. And mercy is a werkyng that comith of the goodnes of God, and it shal lestyn in werkyng al along as synne is suffrid to pursue rythful soule; and whan synne hath no longer leve to pursue, than shal the werkyng of mercy secyn; and than shal al be browte to rythfulhede and therein stondin withoute ende. And by his suffranc we fallyn; and in his blisful love with his myte and his wisdom we are kept; and be mercy and grace we arn reysid to manyfold more ioyes. And thus in rythfulhede and in mercy he wil be knowen and lovid now withoute ende. And the soul that wisely beholdyth it in grace, it is wel plesyd with bothen, and endlesly enioyeth.

36

Of another excellent dede that our lord shal don, which be grace may be k[n]owen[74] a party here, and how we shuld enioyen in the same; and how God yet doith myracles—xxxvi chapter.

Our lord God shewid that a dede shall be done and hymsef shal don it; and I shal do nothyng but synne, and my synne shal not lettyn his goodnes werkyng. And I saw that the beholdyng of this is an heyly[75] ioy in a dredful soule which evermore kyndly be grace desirith Godds wille. This dede shal be begonne here, and it shal be worshipful to God and plentously profitable to his lovers in erth; and ever as we come to heyvyn we sha[lle][76] sen it in mervelous ioye, and it shal lestyn thus in werkyng onto the last day; and the worship and the bliss of that shal lestyn in hevyn aforn God and al his holy without end. Thus was this dede sene and understond in our lords menyng, and the cause why he shewid it is to maken us enioyen in hym and al his werks. Whan I saw his shewing continuid, I understod that it was shewid for a grete thyng that was for to come; which thyng God shewid that hymselfe should don it; which dede hath these properties afornseid; and this shewid wel blisfully, menand that I should take it wysely, feithfully and trostily. But what this dede shuld be, it was kepid privy to me. And in this I saw that he wil not we dredyn to know the thyngs that he shewith; he shewith hem for he will we know hem, be which knowing he will we love hym and lekyn and endlesly enioyen in hym. And for the grete love that he hat to us he shewith us al that is worshipfull and profitable for the tyme; and the thyngs that he will now hav privy, yet of his grete goodness he shewith hem close, in which shewyng he will we leven and understonden that we shal sen it verily in his endles bliss. Than owe we to enioyen in hym

for al that he shewith and al that he hidyth; and if we wilfully
and mekely doe thus, we shal fynd therin gret ese; and endles
thanks we shall have of hym therfore. And thus is the
understondyng of this word: that it shal be don by me—that
is the general man, that is to sey, al that shal be save—it
sha[lle][77] be worshipful and mervelous and plentevous and
God hymself shal don it. And this shal be the heyest ioye that
may ben, to beholden the dede that God hymselfe shal don,
and man shal do ryte nowte but synne. Than menyth our lord
God thus, as if he seid: 'Behold and se. Here hast thou matter
of mekenes; here hast thou matter of love; here hast thou
matter to nowten thyself; her hast thou matter to enioyen in
me; and for my love enioye in me, for of al thyngs, therwith
myte thou most plese me.' And as long as we arn in this lif,
what tyme that we be our folly turne us to the beholdyng of
the reprovyd, tenderly our lord God toucht us and blissfuly
clepyth us, seyand in our soule: 'Lete be al thi love[78] my
dereworthy child. Entend to me, I am enow to the, and enioye
in thi savior and in thi salvation.' And that this is our lo[r]ds[79]
werkyng in us I am sekir; the soule that is aperceyvid therein
be grace shal sen it and felen it. And thow it be so that this
dede be truly taken for the general man, yet it excludith not
the special; for what our good lord will do be his pore
creatures, it is now onknowen to me. But this dede and the
tother afornseid, they arn not both on but ii sundry. But this
dede shal be don[80] sooner, and that shal be as [we][81] come to
hevyn; and to whom our lord gevyth it, it may be knowen her
in party; but the gret dede afornseid, shal nether be knowen
in hevyn ner erth till it is don. And moreover he gave special
vnderstondyng and techyng of werkyng of miracles, as thus:
'It is knowen that I have done miracles her aforn, many and
fele, heygh and mervelous, worshipful and grete; and so as I
have don I do now continualy, and shal don in coming of
tyme.' It is know that afor miracles comen sorow and anguish
and tribulation; and that is that we showld know our owne
febilnes and our myschevis that we arn fallen in by synne to
mekin us and maken us to dreden God, cryen for helpe and
grace. Myracles commen after that, and that of the hey myte,

wisdam and goodnes of God, shewand his vertue and the ioyes
of hevyn so as it may be in this passand life, and that for to
strength our feith and to encresyn our hope, in charite; wherfor
it plesyth hym to be knowen and worshippid in miracles. Than
menyth he thus: he wil that we be not born over low [for][82]
sorrow and tempests that fallen to us; for it hath ever so ben
aforn myracle comyng.

37

*God kepyth his chosen ful sekirly althowe thei synne, for in
these is a godly will that never assayed to synne—xxxvii chapter.*

God browte to my mynd that I shuld synne; and for lykyng
that I had in beholdyng of hym I entended not redily to that
shewyng. And our lord full mercifully abode and gave me
grace to entendyn. And thys shewyng I toke singularly to
myselfe, but be al the gracious comforte that[t][83] folowyth, as
ye shal seen, I was leryd to take it to al my even cristen, al in
general and nothing in special; thowe our lord shewid me I
should synne, by me alone is vnderstode al. And in this I
concyvid a soft drede, and to this our lord answerid: 'I kepe
the ful sekirly.' This word was seid with more love and
sekirness and gostly kepyng than I can or may telle; for as it
was shewid that I should synne, ryth so was the comforte
shewid: sekirnes and kepyng for al myn evyn cristen. What
may make me more to love myn evyn cristen than to seen in
God that he lovyth all that shal be savid as it wer al on soule?
For in every soule that shal be savid is a godly wil that never
assentid to synne ne never shal; ryth as there is a bestly will
in the lower party that may [w]illen[84] no good, ryth so ther is
a godly will in the heyer party, which will is so good that it
may never willen yll but ever good; and therfore we arn that
he lovith, and endlesly we do that that hym lykyt. And
this shewid our lord in the holehede of love that we stonden
in in his syght: ya, that he lovith us now a[s][85] wele whil
we arn here as he shal don whan we arn there afore his blissid

51

face. But for faylyng of love on our party, therefore is al our travel.

38

Also God shewid that synne shal be no shame, but worship to man; for ryth as to every synne is answeryng a peyne be trewth, ryth so, for every synne, to the same soule is goven a bliss by love. Ryth as dyvers synnes arn punyshid with dyvers peynes after that thei be grevous, ryth so shal thei be rewardid with dyvers ioyes in hevyn after thei have be peynful and sorowful to the soule in erthe; for the soule that shal come to hevyn is pretious to God and the place so worshipful that the goodnes of God suffrith never that soul to synne that shal come there, but which synne shal be rewardid; and it is made knowen without end, and blisfully restorid be over passyng worshipps; for in thys syte myn vnderstondyng was lift up into hevyn; and than God browte merily to my minde David and other in the old law without numbre, and in the new law he browte to my mynd first Mary Magdalen, Peter and Paul, and those of Inde[86] and Seynt Iohn of Beverley, and other also without noumbre: how thei are knowen in the church in erth with ther synnes and it is to hem no shame, but al is turnyd hem to worship. And therfore our curtes lord shewith for them here in parte like as it is there in fulhede; for ther the token of synne is turnyd to worshippe. And Seynt Iohn of Beverley, our lord shewid hym ful heyly in comfort to us for homlyhed and browte to my mynde how he is an hende neybor and of our knowyng; and God called hym Seynt Iohn of Beverly pleynly as we doe, and that with a full glad, swete chere shewyng that he is a ful hey seynt in hevyn in his syght, and a blisfull; and with this he made mention that in his youngth and in his tendyr age he was a derworthy servant to God, mekyl God lovand and dredand, and nevertheless God suffrid him to fall, hym mercyfully kepand that he perishid not ne lost no tyme; and afterward God reysyd hym to manyfold more grace, and be the contrition and mekenes that he had in his living God hat goven hym in hevyn manyfold ioyes overpassing that he shuld hav had if he had not fallen. And that thys is soth God shewith in erth with plentivous miracles doyng aboute his body continuly. And al was this to make us glad and mery in love.

39

Of the sharpnes of synne and the godenes of contrition, and how our kynd lord will not we dispair for often fallyng—xxxix chapter.

Synne is the sharpest scorge that any chousyn soule may be smyten with; which scorge al forbetyth man and woman and noyith him in his own syte so ferforth that otherwhile he thynkyth hymself he is not worthy but as to synken in helle til whan contrition takyth hym be touchyng of the Holy Gost and turnyth the bitternes in hopes of Gods mercy; and than he begynnyth his woundis to helyn and the soule to quickkyn tur[n]yd[87] into the life of holy chirch. The Holy Gost ledyth hym to confession wilfully to shewyn his synnes, nakidly and truely, with grete sorow and grete shame that he hath defoulyd the fair ymage of God. Than underfo[n]gyth[88] he penance for every synne, enioynid by his domysman; that is groundid in holy church be the teaching of the Holy Ghost. And this is on mekenes that mekyl plesyt God; and also bodely sekenes of Gods sendyng, and also sorow and shame from withoute, and reprove and dispyte of this world with al manner grevance and temptations that wil[89] be cast in, bodily and gostly. Ful pretiously our lord kepyth us whan it semyth to us that we arn nere forsakyn and cast away for our synne and because we have deservyd it. And because of mekenes that we gettyn hereby we arn reysyd wol hey in Godds syte, be his grace,[90] with so grete contrition, also with compassion and trew longyng to God. Than thei be sodenly delyveryd of synne and of peyne and taken up to bliss and made even hey seynts. Be contrition we arn made clene, be compassion we arn made redy and be trew longyng to God we arn made worthy. Thes arn iii menys, as I understond, wherby that al soulis come to hevyn—that is to seyn, that have ben synners in erth and shal be save—for be these medycines behovyth that every soule be helyd. Thow he be helyd his wounds arn seen aforn God, not as wounds, but as worships. And so on the contrarye wise, as we ben ponishid here with sorow and with penance, we shal be rewardid in hevyn be the curtes love of our lord God almigty that wil that non that come there lose his travel in no degre; for he holdyth synne as sorow and peyne to his lovers in whome he assigneth no blame for love. The mede that we shall underfongyn shal not be litil, but it shal be hey, glorious and worshipfull. And so shal shame be turnyd to worship and more ioye; for our curtes lord wil not that his servants dispeir for often ne for grevous fallyng; for our fallyng lettyth not hym to love us. Peas and love arn ever in us, beand and werkand, but we be not alway in pese and in love; but he wil that we taken hede thus: that he is ground of al our hole life in love, and furthermore that he is our everlestyng keper and mytyly defendith us ageyn our enemys that ben ful fel and fers upon us; and so mech our nede is the more for we gyven hym occasion be our fallyng.

40

Us nedyth to longyn on love with Iesus, eschewyng synne for love; the vyleness of synne passith al peynes, and God lovith wol tenderly us while [we][91] *be in synne, and so us nedyth to doe our neybor—xl chapter.*

This is a severayn frendshyp of our curtes lord that he kepyth us so tenderly whil we be in synne; and furthermore he touchyth us ful privily and shewyth us our synne be the swete lyte of mercy and grace. But whan we seen ourselfe so foule, than wene we that God were wroth with us for our synne, and than aren we steryd of the Holy Gost be contrition into prayers and desire to amendyng of our life with al our mytes, to slakyn the wreth of God, onto the tyme we find a rest in soule and softness in consciens; and than hope we that God hath forgoven us our synnes; and it is soth. And than shewith our curtes lord hymselfe to the soul, wol merily and with glad cher, with frendful welcummyng, as if he had ben in peyn and in prison, sayand swetely thus: 'My derlyng I am glad thou art comen to me. In al thi wo I have ever be with the and now seist thou my lovyng and we be onyd in bliss.' Thus arn synnes forgoven be mercy and grace and our soule worshipfully receivid in ioye, like as it shal be whan it comyth to hevyn, as oftentymes as it comys be the gracious werkyng of the Holy Gost and the vertue of Crists passion. Here vnderstond I sothly that al manner thyng is made redy to us be the grete goodnes of God so ferforth that what tyme we ben ourself in peas and charite we be verily save. But for we may not have this in fulhede whil we arn here, therefore it befallyth us evermore to leven in swete prayor and in lovely longyng with our lord Iesus; for he longyth ever to bryng us to the fulhede of ioy, as it is afornseid where he shewith the gostly threst. But now, because of al this gostly comfort that is afornseyd, if ony man or woman be sterid be foly to seyn or to thinken 'If this be soth, than were it good to synne to have the more mede', or ell to chargyn the less to synne, beware of this steryng, for sothly, if it come it is ontrew and of the enemy of the same trew love that techith us all this comforte. The same blissid love techith us that we should haten synne only for love. And I am sekir, by myn owen felyng, the more that every kinde soul seith this in the curtes love of our lord God, the lother is hym to synne and the more he is ashamid; for if afor us were layd al the peynes in helle and in purgatory and in erth, deth and other, and synne, we shuld rather chose al that peyne than synne; for synne is so vile and so mekyl to haten that it may be liken to no payne—which peyne is not synne. And to me was shewid no herder helle than synne, for a kynde soule hath non helle but synne. And we govyn our intent to love and mekenes, be the werkyng of mercy and grace we arn mad al fair and clene. And as mygty and as wyse as God is to save man, as willy[ng][92] he is; for Criste hymselfe is ground of all the lawis of Cristen men, and he tawth us to doe good ageyn ille. Here may we se that he is hymselfe this charite, and doith to us as he techith us to don; for he will we be like hym in holehede of endless love to ourselfe and to our even cristen. No more than his love is broken to us for our synne, no more will he that our love be broken to ourselfe and to our evyn cristen; but nakidly haten by synne and endlesly loven the soule as God lovith it. Than shal we haten synne lyke as God hatith it, and love the soule as God lovyth it; for this word that [God][93] seid is an endless comfort: 'I kepe the sekirly.'

41

The xiiiith revelation is as afornseyd etc., it is impossible we shuld pray for mercy and want it; and how God will we alway pray thow we be drey and barryn, for that prayer is to him acceptabil and plesante—xli chapter.

After this our lord shewid for prayers; in which shewing I se ii conditions in our lordis menyng: on is rytfulnes, another is sekir troste. But yet oftentymes our troste is not full, for we arn not sekir that God herith us, as us thynkith, for our unworthyness and for we felyn ryth nowte; for we arn as barren and dry oftentymes after our prayors as we wer aforn; and this, in our felyng, our foly, is cause of our wekenes; for thus have I felt in myselfe. And al this browte our lord sodenly to my mend and s[h]ewid[94] these words and seid: 'I am ground of thi besekyng: first it is my wille that thou have it, and sythen I make the to willen it, and sithen I make the to besekyn it and thou besekyst it; how shuld it than be that thou shuld not have thyn besekyng?' And thus in the first reason, with the iii that followen, our good lord shewith a mytye comforte, as it may be seen in the same words. And in the first reason thus he seith: 'And thou besekyst it'; there he shewith ful grete

56

plesance and endles mede that he will gevyn us for our besekyng. And in the vit reason, there he seith 'How shuld it than be? etc.' this was seid for an impossible; for it is most impossible that we shuld besekyn mercy and grace and not have it; for of all thyng that our good lord makyth us to besekyn, hymselfe hath ordeynid it to us from withoute begynnyng. Here may we seen that our besekyng is not cause of Godis goodness; and that shewid he sothfastly in al these swete words when he seith 'I am grounde'. And our good lord wille that this be knowen of his lovers in erth; and the more that we knowen the more shuld we besekyn, if it be wisely taken; and so is our lords menyng. Besekyng is a new, gracious, lestyng will of the soule ony[d]⁹⁵ and festenyd into the will of our lord be the swete, privy werke of the Holy Gost. Our lord hymselfe, he is the first receyvor of our prayors, as to my syte, and takyth it ful thankfully and heyly enioyand; and he sendyth it up aboven and settith it in tresour wher it shal never perishen. It is ther aforn God with al his holy, continuly recyvyd, ever spedand our nedys; and whan we shal under-fongyn our bliss it shal be gevyn us for a degre of ioye with endles worshipful thankyng of hym. Full glad and mery is our lord of our prayors, and he lokyth therafter and he wil have it; for with his grace he makyth us lyke to hymself in condition as we arn in kynd; and so is his blisful will; for he seith thus: 'Pray inderly thow the thynkyth it savowr the nott, for it is profitable thow thou fele it not, thow thou se nowte, ya, thow thou thynke thou myghte nowte; for in dryhede and in barrenhede, in sekenes and in febi[l]hede,⁹⁶ than is thyn prayers wel plesant to me, thow the thynkyth it savowr the nowte but litil. And so is al thy levyng prayers in my syte.' For the mede and the endles thanke that he wil gevyn us, therfore he is covetous to have us pray continuly in his syhte. God acceptith the good will and the travel of his servant, howsoever we felen; wherfore it plesyth hym that we werkyn and in our prayors and in good levyng, be hys helpe and his grace, resonably with discr[e]tion⁹⁷ kepand our myght to hym til whan that we have hym that we sekyn in fulhede of ioy: that is, Iesus. And that shewid he in the [xv],⁹⁸ for aforn, this

word: 'Thou shalt have me to thy mede.' And also to prayors
longyth tha[n]kyng.[99] Thankyng is a new, inward knowing,
with gret reverens and lovely drede turnyng ourselfe with
all our myghts into the werkyng that our good lord steryth us
to, enioyng and thankyng inwardly. And sometyme, for
plenteoushede, it brekyth out with voyce and seith: 'Good
lord, grante mercy; blissid mot thou be!' And sumtyme whan
the herte is drey and felyth not, or ell be temptation of our
enemy, than it is dreven by reason and be grece to cryen upon
our lord with voyce, rehersyng his blissid passion and his gret
goodnes. And the vertue of our lords word turnyth into the
soule and quicknith the herte and entrith it be his grace into
trew werkyng, and makyth it prayen wel blisfully and trewly
to enioyen our lord; it is a ful blisful thankyng in his syte.

42

*Off iii thyngs that longyn to prayor, and how we shuld pray;
and of the goodnes of God that supplyeth alwey our imperfection and febilnes whan we do that longyth to us to do—xlii
chapter.*

Our lord God wille we have trew understondyng, and namely
in iii thyngs that longyn to our prayors. The first is be whom
and how that our prayors springyth; be whome he shewith
when he seith 'I am ground'; and how, be his goodness, for
he seith 'First it is my wille'. For the secund, in what manner
and how we should usen our prayors; and that is that our wil
be turnyd into the will of our lord, enioyand: and so menith
he whan he seith 'I mak the to willen it'. For the thred, that
we knowen the frute and the end of our prayors: that is, to
be onyd and lyk to our lord in althyng. And to this menyng
and for this end was al this lovely lesson shewid; and he wil
helpyn us and we shall make it so as he seith hymselfe—blissid
mot he ben! For this is our lords wille, that our prayors and
our troste ben both alyk large; for if we trost not as mekyl as
we preyen, we doe not ful worship to our lord in our prayors

and also we taryen and peyn ourselfe; and the cause is, as I
leve, for we know not truly that our lord is ground on whom
our prayors springith, and also that we know not that it is
goven us be the grace of his love; for if we knew this it would
maken us to trosten to hav, of our lords gyfte, al that we desire;
for I am sekir that no man askyth mercy and grace with trew
menyng, but mercy and grace be first geyvin to hym. But
sumtyme it cumyth to our mynd that we have prayd long tyme,
and yet, thynkyth us, that we have not our askyng; but herfor
should we not be hevy; for I am sekir, be our lords menyng,
that eyther we abyden a better tyme, or more grace, or a better
gyfte. He will we have trow knowyng in hymself that he is
beyng; and in this knowyng he will that our vnderstondyng be
growndid with al our mytys and al our entent and al our
menyng; and in this grownd he will that we taken our stede
and our wonynge. And be the gracious ligte of hymself he will
we have understondyng of the thyngs that folow: the first is
our noble and excellent makyng; the second, our pretious and
derworthy agen byeing; the thred, althyng that he hath made
benethen us to serven us and, for our love, kepith it. Than
menyth he thus, as if he seyd: 'Behold and se that I have don
al this beforn thi prayors, and now thou art and prayest me.'
And thus he menyth that it longyth to us [to]¹⁰⁰ wetyn that
the gretest deds be don, as holy church techyth. And in the
beholdyng of thys with thankyng we owte to pray for the dede
that is now in doyng: and that is that he reule us and gyde us
to his worshippe in thys lif and bryng us to his bliss; and
therfore he hath don all. Than menyth he thus: that sen that
he doth it and we prayen therfor; for that on is not enow; for
if we prayen and sen not that he doth it, it makyth us hevy
and doutful, and that is not his worshippe. And if we sen that
he doth, and we pray not, we do not our dette; and so may it
not ben, that is to seyen, so is it not in his beholdyng; but to
sen that he doth it and to pray forthwith, so is he worshippid
and we sped. Althyng that our lord hath ordeynyd to don, it
is his will that we prayen therfor, other in specyal or in
generall; and the ioy and the bliss that it is to hym, and the
thanke and the worshippe that we shall have therfore, it

59

passyth the vnderstondyng of cretures, as to my syte; for prayor is a rythwis vnderstondyng of that fulhede of ioye that is for to cume, with wel longyng and sekir troste. Faylyng of our bliss that we ben kyndly ordeynid to makyth us for to longen; trew vnderstondyng and love, with swete mynd in our savior, graciously makyth us for to trosten. And in these ii werkyngs our lord beholdyth us continuly; for it is our dett, and his goodnes may no less assignen in us. Than longyth it to us to don our diligens; and whan we have don it, than shal us yet thinken that is nowte—and soth it is. But do we as we may, and sothly aske mercy and grace, al that us faylyth we shal fynd in hym; and thus menyth he wher he seith: 'I am grounde of thy besekyng.' And thus in this blisful word, with the shewing, I saw a full overcomyng agens al our wekenes and al our douteful dredis.

43

What prayor doth, ordeynyd to God will; and how the goodnes of God hath gret lekyng in the deds that he doth be us, as he wer beholden to us, werkyng althyng ful swetely—xliii chapter.

Prayor onyth the soule to God; for thow the soule be ever lyke to God in kynde and substance, restorid be grace, it is often onlyke in condition be synne on manys partye. Than is prayor a wittnes that the soule will as God will, and comfortith the conscience and ablith man to grace. And thus he techith us to prayen, and mytyly to trosten that we shal have it; for he beholdith us in love and wil makyn us partyner of his gode dede, and therfore he steryth us to prayen that that likyth hym to don; for which prayors and gode will that he[101] wil have of his gyft he wil reward us and gevyn us endless mede. And this was shewid in this word: 'And thou besekyst it.' In this word God shewid so gret plesance and so gret lykyng, as he were mekyl beholden to us for every god dede that we don—and yet it is he that doth it—and for that we besekyn hym mytyly

to don althyng that hym lekyt; as if he seid: 'What myte then
plese me more than to besekyn mytyly, wisely and wilfully to
do that thyng that I shal don?' And thus the soule be prayor
accordyth to God. But whan our curtes lord of his grace[102]
shewith hymse[l]fe[103] to our soule, we have that we desire;
and than we se not for the tyme what we shuld pray, but al
our entent with al our myte is sett holy to the beholdyng of
hym; and this is an hey, onperc[ey]vable[104] prayor, as to my
syte; for al the cause wherfor we prayen, it is onyd into the
syte and beholdyng of hym to whome we prayen, mervelously
enioyand with reverent drede and so grete sweteness and
delite in hym that we can pray ryth nowte but as he steryth
us for the tyme. And wel I wote the mor the soule seeth of
God, the more it desyrith hym be his grace. But whan we sen
hym not so, than fele we nede and cause to pray—for
faylyng—for ablyng[105] of ourselfe to Iesus; for whan the soule
is tempested, troublid and left to hymself be onreste, than it
is tyme to prayen to maken hymselfe supple and buxum to
God. But he be no manner of prayor makyth God supple to
hym, for he is ever alyke in love. And thus I saw that what
tyme we se nedys wherfore we prayen, than our good lord
folowyth us, helpand our desire. And whan we of his special
grace planely beholden hym, seying non other nedys, than we
folowen hym and he drawith us into hym be love; for I saw
and felt that his mervelous and fulsome goodnes fulfillith al
our mytys; and then I saw that his continuate werkyng in al
manner thing is don so godely, so wysely and so mytyly that
it overpassyt al our imagynyng and all that we can wenyn and
thynken; and than we can do no more but behold hym,
enioyeng, with an hey migty desire to be al onyd into hym,
centered to his wonyng, and enioy in hys lovyng and deliten
in his godeness. And then shal we, with this swete grace, in
our owen meke continuat prayors, come into him now in thys
life be many privy tuchyngs of swete gostly syghts and felyng,
mesurid to us as our simplehede may bere it; and this [is][106]
wrewte, and shal be, be the grace of the Holy Gost, so long
til we shal dey in longyng for love. And than shal we all come
into our lord, ourselfe clerely knowand and God fulsomely

havyng; and we endlesly ben al had in God, hym verily seand and fu[l]sumly[107] feland, hym gostly heryng, and hym delectably smellyng and hym swetely swelowyng; and than shal we sen God face to face, homly and fulsumly; the creature, that is made, shal sen and endlesly beholden God, which is the maker; for thus may no man sen God and leven after, that is to sey, in this dedly life; but whan he of his special grace wil shewn him here, he st[r]engtneth[108] the creature above the selfe, and he mesurith the shewing after his own wille, as it is profitable for the tyme.

44

Of the properties of the Trinite; and how mannys soule, a creature, hath the same properties, doyng that that it was mede for, seyng, beholdyng and mervelyng his God; so, by that, it semyth as nowte to the selfe—xliiii chapter.

God shewid in al the revelations oftentymes that man werkyth evermore his will and his wership lestyngly withoute ony styntyng. And what this worke is was shewid in the first, and that in a mervelous grounde, for it was shewid in the werkyng of the soule of our blisfull lady Seynt Mary, treuth and wisdam; and how, I hope be the grace of the Holy Gost I shal say as I saw. Treuth seith God, and wisedam beholdyth God, and of these ii comyth the thred: that is an holy mervelous delyte in God, which is love. Wher treuth and wisdam is verily, there is love verily commond of hem bothyn, and al of God makyng; for he is endles soverain trueth, endles severeyn wisdam, endles sovereyn love, onmade; and man soule is a creature in God, which hath the same propertyes made; and evermore it doith that it was made for: it seith God, it beholdyth God and it lovyth God; wherof God enioyith in the creature, and the creature in God, endlesly mervelyng; in which mervelyng he seith his God, his lord, his maker, so hey, so gret and so good in reward of hym that is made, that onethys the creature semyth owte to the selfe; but the cleryte and the clenes of

treuth and wisdam makyth hym to sen and to beknowen that
he is made for love; in which God endlesly kepyth him.

45

Of the ferme and deepe iugement of God and the variant
iugement of man—xlv chapter.

God demyth us upon our kynde substance which is ever kept
on in hym, hoole and save without end; and this dome is
of his rythfulhede. And man iugith upon our changeabil
sensualyte which semyth now on, now other, after that it takyth
of the parties, and shewyth outward. And this wisdam is
medyllid; for sumtyme it is good and esye, and sumtyme it
[is]¹⁰⁹ herd and grevous. And in as mekil as it is good and esy
it longyth to the rythfulhede; and in as mekyl as it is herd and
grevous, our good lord Iesus reformyth it be mercy and grace
throw the vertue of his blissid passion, and so bryngith into
the rythfulhede. And thow these ii be thus accordid and onyd,
yet it shal be knowen, both, in hevyn without end. The first
dome, which is of God rythfulhed, and that is of his hey,
endless life; and this is that faire swete dome that was shewid
in al the fair revelation in which I saw him assigne to us no
manner of blame. And thow this was swete and delectabil, yet
only in the beholdyng of this I cowd nowte be full esyd, and
that was for the dome of holy church which I had aforn
vnderstond and was continuly in my syte. And therfore be this
dome methowte me behovyd neds to know me a synner, and
be the same dome I understode that synners arn worthy
sumtime blame and wreth; and these ii cowth I not se in God,
and there my desir was more than I can or may tell; for the
heyer dome God shewid hymselfe in the same tyme, and
therfore me behovyd neds to taken it; and the lower dome
was lern me aforn in holy church, and therfore I myte in no
way levyn the lower dome. Than was this my desire: that I
myte sen in God in what manner that the dome of holy church
herin techyth is trew in his syte, and how it longyth to me

sothly to knoyn it; wherby thei myte both be savid; so as it wer worshipfull to God and ryte way to me. And to al this I had non other answere but a mervelous example of a lord and of a servant, as I shal seyn after, and that ful mytyly[110] shewid. And yet I stond in desire, and will into my end, that I myte be grace knowen thes ii domys as it longyth to me; for al hevynly, and al erthly things that longyn to hevyn, arn comprehendid in these ii domys. And the more vnderstondyng be the gracious ledyng of the Holy Gost that we have of these ii domys, the more we shal sen and known our faylyngs. And ever the more that we sen hem, the more kynd[l]y[111] be grace we shal longen to be fulfillid of endles ioye and bliss; for we arn made therto, and our kindly substance is now blisful in God, and hath be sithen it was made, and shall, without end.

46

We cannot knowen ourself in this life but be feith and grace, but we must know ourself synners; and how God is never wreth, being most nere the soule, it kepyng—xlvi chapter.

But our passand lif that we have here in our sensualite knowith not what ourself is;[112] than shal we verily and clerly sen and knowen our lord God in fulhede of ioy. And therfore it behovyth neds to be that the nerer we be our bliss, the more we shall longen, and that both be kynd and be grace. We may have knowing of ourselfe in this life be continuant helpe and vertue of our hey kynd, in which knowing we may encrecin and wexen be [fortheryng][113] and speding of mercy and grace, but we may never full know ourselfe into the laste poynte; in which poynte this passend life and manner of peyne and wo shall have an end. And therfore it longyth properly to us, both be kynd and be grace, to longen and desiren with al our myghts to knowen ourselfe[114] in fulhede of endles ioye. And yet in al this tyme, from the begynnyng to the end, I had ii manner of beholdyng; that one was endless continuant love with sekirnes of kepyng and blisful salvation, for of this was al the shewing;

that other was the common techyng of holy church in which
I was aforn enformyd and growndid, and wilfully haveing in
use and understondyng. And the beholdyng of this come not
from me; for be the shewing I was not sterid ne led therfrom
in no manner poynte, but I had therin teching to loven it and
liken it, wherby I myte, be the helpe of our lord and his grace,
encrecy and resyn to more hevynly knowyng and heyer
lovyng. And thus in al this beholdyng methowte it behovyd
nedys to sen and to knowen that we arn synners, and don
many evill that we owten to leven, and levyn many good dedes
ondon that we owten to don, wherfore we deserve peyne and
wreth. And notwithstondyng al this I saw sothfastly that our
lord was never wreth ne never shall, for he is God: good, life,
trueth, love, peas; his charite and his unite suffrith hym not
to be wroth; for I saw trewly that it is agens the properte of
myte to be wroth, and agens the properte of his wisdam and
agens the properte of his goodnes. God is the goodnes that
may not be wroth for he is not but goodnes; our soule [is][115]
vnyd to hym, onchangable goodnes, and betwix God and our
soule is neyther wroth nor forgifenes in his syte; for our soule
is fulsomly onyd to God of his owen goodnes, that atwix God
and soule may ben ryth nowte. And to this vnderstondyng
was the soul led by love and drawne be mygte in every
shewing; that it is thus our good lord shewid and how it is thus
sothly of his gret goodnes; and he will we desire to wetyn, that
is to seyn, as it longyth to his creature to wetyn it; for althyng
that the simple soule understode God will that it be shewid
and knowen; for the thyngs that he will have privy, mytyly
and wisely hymselfe he hydeth hem for love; for I saw in the
same shewing that mech privity is hid which may never be
knowen into the tyme that God of his goodnes hath made us
worthy to sen it. And therwith I am wele paid, abyding our
lords will in this hey mervel. And now I yeele me to my moder
holy church as a simple child owyth.

47

*We must reverently mervelyn and mekly suffren, ever enioyand
in God; and how our blyndhede in that we se not God is cause
of synne—xlvii chapter.*

Tweyn poynts longen to our soule be dett: on is that we
reverently mervelyn, that other is that we mekly suffryn, ever
enioyand in God; for he will we wetyn that we shal in short
tyme se clerly in hymself al that we desire. And notwithstondyng al this I beheld and mervelyd gretly what is the mercy
and forgivenes of God; for be the techyng that I had aforn, I
understode that the mercy of God shuld be the forgevenes of
his wreth after the tyme that we have synned; for methowte,
to a soule whose menyng and desire is to loven, that the wreth
of God wer herder than any other peyne, and therfor I toke
that the forgeveness of his wreth shuld be one of the principal
poynts of his mercy. But for nowte that I myte beholden and
desyrin I could no se this poynte in al the shewyng. But how
I understode and saw of the werks of mercy I shal sey sumdel,
as God wil geve me grace. I understode this man is chongeable
in this lif, and be frelte and overcummyng[116] fallith into synne;
he is onmytye and onwise of hymself, and also his wil is
overleyd; and in this tyme he is in tempest and in sorow and
wo, and the cause is blindhede, for he seith not God; for if he
sey God continuly he shuld have no mischevous felyng, ne no
manner steryng the yernyng that servyth to synne. Thus saw
I and felt in the same tyme; and methowte that the syte and
the felyng was hey and plentivous and gracious in reward that
our commen felyng is in this lif; but yet I thowte it was
but smal and low in reward of the great desire that the soule
hath to sen God. For I felt in me v manner of werkyngs which
be these: enioying, morning, desir, drede and sekir hope;
enioyeng, for God gave me vnderstondyng and knowing that
it was hymself that I saw; morning, and that was for faylyng;
desir, and that was that I myte sen hym ever more and more,

vnderstondyng and knowyng that we shal never have ful rest til we sen hym verily and clerly in hevyn; drede was for it semyd to me in al that tyme that that syte shuld fayle and I ben left to myselfe; sekir hope was in the endles love, that I saw I shuld be kept be his mercy and browte to his bliss. And the ioyeing in his syte with this sekir hope of his mercyful kepyng made me to have felyng and comforte so that morneing and drede were not gretly peynfull. And yet in al this I beheld in the shewing of God that this manner syte of him may not be continuant in this lif, and that for his owen worship and for encreas of our endles ioy. And therefore we failen oftentymes of the syte of hym, and anon we fallen into ourself, and than fynde we no felyng of ryth—nowte but contrarioust that is in ourselfe, and that of the elder rote of our first synne with all that followyn of our contrivans, and in this we arn traveylid and tempestid with felyng of synnys and of peynes in many dyvers manner, gostly and bodyly, as it [is]¹¹⁷ knowen to us in this lif.

48

Off mercy and grace and their propertyes; and how we shall enioy that ever we suffrid wo patiently—xlviii chapter.

But our good lord the Holy Gost, which is endles lif wonnyng in our soule, ful sekirly kepyth us, and werkyth therin a peas and bryngith it to ese be grace and accordith it to God and makyth it buxum. And this is the mercy and the wey that our lord continuly ledyth us in as longe as we ben here in this lif which is chongeabile; for I sow no wreth but in mannys partie, and that forgevyth he in us; for wreth is not ell but a frowardness and a contrarioste to peace and to love, and eyther it commyth of faylyng of myte or of faylyng of wisdam, or of faylyng of goodnes, which faylyng is not in God, but it is on our partie; for we be synne and wretchidnes have in us a wretchid and continuant contrariuste to peace and to love, and that shewid he full often in his lovely chere of ruth and

67

pety; for the ground of mercy is love, and the werkyng of mercy is our kepyng in love; and this was shewid in swich manner that I cowth not aperceyven of the partye of mercy otherwise but as it were alone in love, that is to sey, as to my syte. Mercy is a swete gracious werkyng in love medilyd with plentevous pitte; for mercy werkith, us kepand, and mercy werkyth turnyng to us althyng to good. Mercy be love suffrith us to faylen be mesur; and in as mech as we faylen, in so mekyl we fallen, and in as mekyl as we fallen, so mekyl we dyen; for us behovyth nedes to deyen in as mech as we failen syght and felyng of God that is our lif. Our faylyng is dredful, ovr falling is shamefull and our deyng is sorowfull; but in al this the swete eye of pite and love cummyth never of us, ne the werkyng of mercy cessyth not. For I beheld the properte of mercy and I beheld the properte of grace, which have ii manner werkyng in one love; mercy is a pitifull propirte which longyth to the moderid in tendyr love, and grace is a worshipful propirte which longith to the ryal lordshipp in the same love; mercy werkyth: keypng, suffring, quecknyng and helyng, and al is of tendernes of love; and grace werkyth: reysing, rewardyng and endlessly overpassyng that our lovyng and our travel deservyth, spreding abrode and shewyng the hey, plentivous largess of Godds ryal lordship in his mervelous curtesye; and this is of the abundance of love; for grace werkyth our dredfull faylyng into plentivous endles solace, and grace werkyth our shamefull fallyng into hey worship reysyng, and grace werkyth our sorowfull deying into holy blisfull lif; for I saw full sekirly that ever as our contrarioust werkyth to us here in erth peyne, shame and sorow, ryth so on the contrariewise, grace werkyth to us in hevyn, solace, worship and bliss; and overpassyng so ferforth that whan we cum up and receivyn the swete reward which grace hath wrowte to us, than we shal thankyn and blissyn our lord, endlesly enioyand that ever we suffrid wo. And that shal be for a properte of blissid love that we shall know in God, which we myte never a knowen withoute wo goeing afore. And whan I saw all this, me behovid nedis to granten that the mercy of God and the forgiveness is to slaken and wasten our wreth.

68

49

*Our lif is growndid in love, withoute the which we perish; but
yet God is never wroth, but in our wreth and synne he mercifully
kepith us and tretith us to peace, rewarding our tribulations
—xlix chapter.*

For this was an hey mervel to the soule, which was continuly
shewid in al, and with gret diligens beholden: that our lord
God, anempts hymself, may not forgevyn, for he may not be
wroth—it were impossible. For this was shewid: that lif is all
groundid and rotid in love, and without love we may not levyn;
and therfore to the soule that of his special grace seyth so
ferforth of the hey mervelous godenes of God, and that we
arn endlesly onyd to hym in love, it is the most impossible
that may ben that God shuld be wreth, for wreth and frendship
be ii contraries; for he that westeth and destroyith our wreth
and makyth us meke and mylde, it behovyth neds to ben that
he be ever on in love, meke and myld, which is contrarious
to wreth; for I saw ful sekirly that wher our lord apperith peas
is taken and wreth hath no place; for I saw no manner of wreth
in God, neyther for short tyme ne for longe, for sothly, as to
my syte, if God myte be wroth a touch we shuld never have
lif ne stede ne beyng; for verily as we have our beyng of the
endles myte of God and of the endless wisdam and of the
endless godeness, as verily we have our kepyng in the endles
myte of God in the endles wisdom and in the endless goodnes;
for thow we felyn in us wretches, debates and strives, yet arn
we al mannerfull[118] beclosyd in the mildhede of God and in
his mekehede in his benignite and in his buxumhede; for I
saw full sekirly that al our endles frendship, our stede, our lif
and our beyng is in God; for that same endles goodnes that
kepith us whan we synne that we perish not, the same endles
goodnes continuly tretyth in us a peace [agaynst][119] our wreth
and our contrarious fallyng and makyth us to sen our nede
with a trew drede mytyly to sekyn into God to have forgivenes

with a gracious desire of our salvation, for we may not be blisfully save til we be verily in peace and in love; for that is our salvation. And thow we, be the wreth and the contrariouste that is in us, be now in tribulation, desese and wo, as fallyth to our blindnes and frelte, yet arn we sekirly safe be the mercifull kepyng of God that we perish not. But we arn not blisfully saf in havyng of our endles ioy till we ben al in peace and in love: that is to sey, ful plesid with God and with al his werks and with al his domys, and lovand and pessible with ourselfe and with our even cristen and with al that God lovith, as love likyth. And this doeth Gods goodnes in us. Thus saw I that God is our very peace and he is our sekir keper whan we arn ourse[l]fe[120] at onpeace, and he continuly werkith to bring us into endles peas. And thus whan we, be the werkyng of mercy and grace, be made meke and mylde, we arn ful safe. Sodenly is the soule onyd to God whan it is trewly pesid in the selfe, for in him is fonden no wreth. And thus I saw, whan we arn all in peace and in love we fynde no contrariouste ne no manner of lettyng of that contrariouste which is now in us. Our lord of his goodnes makyth it to us ful profitable; for that contrarioust is cause of our tribulations and al our wo, and our lord Iesus takyth hem and send hem up to hevyn, and there arn thei made more swete and delectable than herte may thynken or tongue may tellen, and whan we cu[m][121] thither we shal fynd hem redy, al turnyd into very faire and endless worships. Thus is God our stedfast ground, and he shal be our full bliss and make us on-chongeable as he is, whan we arn there.

50

How the chosen soule was never ded in the syte of God, and of a mervel upon the same; and iii things boldid hir to aske of God the vnderstondyng of it—l chapter.

And in this dedly lif mercy and forgivenes is our wey and evermore ledyth us to grace. And be the tempest and the

sorow that we fallen in on our parte, we be often dede, as to
manys dome in erth, but in the syte of God the soule that shal
be save was never dede ne never shall. But yet here I wondrid
and mervelid with al the diligens of my soul menand thus:
'Good lord, I se the that art very truth and I know sothly that
we synne grevously al day and ben mekyl blameworthy; and
I ne may neyther levyn the k[n]owyng[122] of this sothe, ner I
ne se the shewyn to us no manner of blame. How may this
be?' For I knew be the common techyng of holy church and
be myne owne felyng that the blame of our synne continuly
hangith upon us, from the first man into the tyme that we
come up into hevyn; than was this my mervel, that I saw our
lord God shewand to us no more blame than if we were as
clene as holy as angelys be in hevyn. And atwix these ii
contraries my reason was gretly traveylid by my blyndhede,
and cowde have no rest for drede that his blyssid presens shuld
passyn from my syte and I to be left in onknowyng how he
beholdyth us in our synne; for either behovid me to sen in
God that synne were al don away, or ell me behovid to sen
in God how he seith it, wherby I myte trewly knowen how it
longyth to me to se synne and the manner of our blame. My
longyn indurid, hym continuly beholding, and yet I cowde
have no patience for great awer and perplexitie, thynkand: 'If
I take it thus, that we be not synners ne no blameworthy, it
semyth as I shuld eryn and faile of knoweing of this soth. And
if it be so that we be synners and blameworthy, good lord,
how may it than ben that I cannot sen this sothnes in the,
which art my God, my maker, in whom I desire to sen al
trueths? For iii poynts makyn me herdy to ask it: the first is
for it is so low a thyng, for if it wer an hey I should ben adred;
the ii is that it is so common, for if it were special and privye,
also I shuld ben adred; the iii is that it nedyth me to wetyn
it, as me thynkyth, if I shall levyn here, for knowyng of
good and evill, wherby I may be reason and grace the more
depart hem on sundre, and loven goodnes and haten evill as
holy church techyth.' I cryed inwardly with al my myte, sekyng
into God for helpe, menand thus: 'A! lord Iesus, king of bliss,
how shall I ben esyd? Ho that shal techyn me and tellen me

that me nedyth to wetyn, if I may not at this tyme sen it in the?'

51

The answere to the doute afor by a mervelous example of a lord and a servant; and God will be abidyn, for it was nere xx yeres after ere she fully vnderstode this example; and how it is vnderstod that Crist syttith on the ryth hand of the Father—li chapter.

And than our curtes lord answerd in shewing full mystily a wonderful example of a lord that hath a servant, and gave me syte to my vnderstondyng of botyrn; which syte was shewid double in the lord, and the syte was shewid dowble in the servant: than on partie was shewid gostly in bodily lyknes, and the other partie was shewid more gostly without bodyly lyknes. For the first thus: I saw ii persons in bodily likenes, that is to sey, a lord and a servant; and therewith God gave me gostly understondyng. The lord sittith solemnly in rest and in peace, the servant standyth by, aforn his lord reverently, redy to don his lords will. The lord lookyth upon his servant ful lovely and swetely, and mekely he sendyth hym to a certain place to don his will. The servant, not only he goeth, but suddenly he stirtith and rynnith in grete haste for love to don his lords will. And anon he fallith in a slade and takith ful grete sore. And than he gronith and monith and waylith and writhith, but he ne may rysen ne helpyn hymself be no manner wey. And of all this the most myscheif that I saw him in was faylyng of comforte; for he cowde not turne his face to loke upon his loving lord, which was to hym ful nere, in whom is ful comfort; but as a man that was febil and onwise for the tyme, he entended to his felyng, and induryd in wo, in which wo he suffrid vii grete peynes. The first was the sore brosyng [that]^[123] he toke in hys fallyng, which was to hym felable peyne. The ii was the hevynes of his body. The iii was febilnes folowyng of these twe. The iiii, that he was blinded in his reason and

72

stonyed in his mend so ferforth that almost he had forgotten his owne luf. The v was that he myte not rysen. The vi was most mervelous to me, and that was that he lay alone; I lokid al aboute and beheld, and fer ne nere, hey ne low, I saw to him no helpe. The vii was that the place which he lay on was a lang, herd and grevous. I merveled how this servant myte mekely suffren there al this wo. And I beheld with avisement to wetyn if I cowth perceyve in hym any defaute, or if the lord shuld assigne in hym any blame, and sothly ther was non seen; for only his good will and his grete desire was cause of his fallyng; and he was as onlothful and as good inwardly as whan he stode afor his lord redy to don his wille. And ryth thus continualy his lovand lord ful tenderly beholdyth him; and now with a double cher; on outward, ful mekely and myldely with grete ruth and pety, and this was of the first; another inward, more gostly, and this was shewid with a ledyng of my vnderstondyng into the lord, which I saw hym heyly enioyen, for the worshipful resting and nobleth that he will and shall bryng his servant to be his plentevous grace, and this was of that other shewyng; and now my vnderstondyng led agen into the first, both kepand in mynd. Than seith this curtes lord in his menyng: 'Lo, lo, my lovid servant. What harme and disese he hath takeyn in my service for my love, ya, and for his good will! Is it not skyl that I award hym his afray and his drede, his hurt and his mai[m]e[124] and al his wo? And not only this, but fallith it not to me to gevyn a geft that be better to hym and more worshipfull than his own hole shuld have ben? And ell me thynkyth I dede hym no grace.' And in this an inward gostly shewing of the lords menyng descendid into my soule, in which I saw that it behovith neds to ben, stondyng his grete and his own worship, that his dereworthy servant which he lovid so mech shuld ben verily and blisfully rewardid without end aboven that he shuld a ben if he had not fallen; ya, and so ferforth that his fallyng and his wo that he hath taken therby shall be turnyd into hey and overpassing worship and endles bliss. And at this poynte the shewing of the example vanishid, and our good lord led forth myn vnderstondyng in syte and in shewing of the revelation to the end. But notwithstondyng al this forthledyng, the mervelyng of the example cam never from me; for methowth it was goven me for an answere to my desir, and yet cowth I not taken therin ful vnderstondyng to myn ese at that tyme; for in the servant that was shewid for Adam, as I shal seyn, I saw many dyvers properties that myten be no manner way ben aret to single Adam. And thus in that tyme I stode mekyl in onknowyng; for the full vnderstondyng of this mervelous example was not goven me in that tyme; in which mystye example iii propertes of the revelation be yet mekyl hidde, and notwithstondyng this I saw and understode that every shewing is full of privities, and therfore me behovith now to tellen iii propertes in which I am sumdele esyd. The frest is the begynnyng of techyng that I understod therein in the same tyme; the ii is the inward lernyng that I have vnderstodyn therein sithen; the iii al the hole revelation from the begynnyng to the end, that is to sey, of this boke, which our lord God of his goodnes bryngeth oftentymes frely to the syte of myn vnderstondyng. And these iii arn so onyd, as to my vnderstondyng, that I cannot, ner may, depart them. And be these iii as on I have techyng wherby I owe to leyvyn and trostyn in our lord God, that of the same godenes that he shewed it, and for the same end, ryth so of the same goodnes and for the same end he shal declaryn it to us whan it is his wille. For xx yeres after the tyme of the shewing, save iii monethis, I had techyng inwardly, as I shal seyen: 'It longyth to the to taken hede to all the propertes and condition that weryn shewid in the example thow thou thynke that they ben mysty and indifferent to thy syte.' I assend wilfully with grete desire [seeing][125] inwardly with avisement al the poynts and propertes that wer shewid in the same tyme, as ferforth as my witt and vnderstondyng wold servyn; begynning myn beholdyng at the lord and at the servant, and the manner of sytting of the lord, and the place that he sate on, and tho color of his clothyng and the manner of shapp, and his cher withouten, and his nobleth and his godenes within; at the manner of stondyng of the servant and the place wher and how, at his manner of clothyng, the color and the shappe, at his outward havyng and at his inward goodnes and his

74

onlothfulhede. The lord that sate solemnly in rest and in peace, I understond that he is God. The servant that stode aforn the lord, I understode that it was shewid for Adam, that is to seyen, on man was shewid that tyme, and his fallyng, to maken that therby understonden how God beholdith a[126] man and his fallyng; for in the syte of God al man is on man and on man is all man. This man was hurte in hys myte and made ful febil; and he was stonyed in his vnderstondyng, for he turnyd from the beholdyng of his lord. But his will was kept hole in God sygte; for his will I saw our lord commenden and approven, but hymselfe was lettid and blindhed of the knowing of this will, and this is to him grete sorow and grevous disese; for neither he seith clerly his lovyng lord, which is to him ful meke and mylde, ne he seith trewly what himself is in the sygte of his lovyng lord. And wel I wote, when these ii are wysely and treuly seyn, we shall gettyn rest and peas her in parte, and the fulhede of the bliss of hevyn, be his plentivous grace. And this was a begynnyng of techyng which I saw in the same tyme wherby I myte com to k[n]owing[127] in what manner he beholdyth us in our synne. And than I saw that only paynys blamith and punishith, and our curtis lord comfortith and sorowith,[128] ever he is to the soule in glad cher, lovand and longand to brynen us to bliss. The place that our lord sat on was symple, on the erth barren and desert, alone in wildernes. His clothyng was wide and syde, and ful semely as fallyth to a lord; the color of his cloth was blew as asure, most sad and fair. His cher was merciful, the color of his face was faire browne with fulsomely featours; his eyen were blak, most faire and semely, shewand ful of lovely pety; and within him an hey ward, longe and brode, all full of endles hevyns. And the lovely lokeing that he loked upon his servant continuly, and namely in his fallyng, methowte it myte molten our herts for love and bresten hem on to for ioy. The fair lokyng shewid of a semely medlur which was mervelous to beholden: that on was ruth and pety, that other was ioye and bliss. The ioy and bliss passith as fer reuth and pite as hevyn is aboven erth. The pite was erthly and the blis was hevenly. The ruth in the pite of [the][129] Fadir was of the falling of Adam,

which is his most lovyd creatur: the ioy and the bliss was of
his dereworthy Son, which is evyn with the Fadir. The merciful
beholdyng of his lofly cher fulfilled al erth and descendid
downe with Adam into helle, with which continuant pite Adam
was kept from endles deth. And this mercy and pite dwellyth
with mankind into the tyme we com up into hevyn. But man
is blindid in this life, and therfore we may not sen our Fader,
God, as he is. And what tyme that he of his goodnes will
shewin hym to man, he shewith him homley as man; notwithstonding[130] I ne saw sothly, we owen to knowen and levyn
that the Fader is not man. But his sitting on the erth barreyn
and desert is this to menyn: he made mans soule to ben his
owen cyte and his dwellyng place, which is most plesyng to
hym of al his werks; and what tyme that man was fallen into
sorow and peyne he was not al semly to servyn of that noble
office; and therfore our kind Fader wold adyten him no other
place but sitten upon the erth abeydand mankynd, which is
medlid with erth, till what time be his grace his derworthy Son
had bowte ageyn his cyte into the noble fayrhede with is herd
travel. The blewhede of the clothing betokinith his stedfastnes.
The brownhede of his fair face with the semely blakhede of
the eyen was most accordyng to shew his holy sobirnes. The
larghede of his clothyng, which were fair, flamand abowten,
betokenith that he hath beclesid in hym a[ll][131] hevyns and al
ioy and blis. And this was shewid in a touch wher I sey 'Myn
vnderstondyng was led into the lord', in which I saw him heyly
enioyen for the worshipful restoring that he wil and shal bring
his servant to be his plenteous grace. And yet I mervellyd,
beholdyng the lord and the servant afornseid. I saw the lord
sitten solemnly, and the servant stondand reverently aforn his
lord, in which servant is double understondyng: on withouten,
another within. Outward, he was clad simply as a labourer
which wer disposid to travel, and he stode ful nere the lord,
not even fornempts hym, but in partie asyd, that on the lift.
His clothyng was a white kirtle, sengil, old and al defacid, died
with swete of his body, streyte fittyng to hym and short, as it
were an handful benethe the knee, bar, semand as it shuld
sone be weryd up, redy to be raggid and rent. And in this I

mervelid gretly thynkand: 'This is now an onsomely clothyng for the servant that is so heyly lovid to stondyn afor so worship lord.' And inward, in him was shewid a ground of love, which love he had to the lord was even like to the love that the lord had to hym. The wisdam of the servant saw inwardly that ther was one thing to don which shuld be to the worshipp of the lord. And the servant for love, haveing no reward to hymselfe ne to nothing that might fallen on him, hastely he stirt and ran at the sendyng of his lord to don that thing which was his will and his worship. For it semyd be his outward clothyng as he had ben a continuant labourer of leng tyme; and be the inward syte that I had, both in the lord and in the servant, it semyd that he was anew, tha[t][132] is to sey, new begynnyng to travellyn, which servant was never sent out aforn. Ther was a tresor in the erth which the lord lovid. I mervelid and thowte what it myte ben. And I was answered in myn vnderstondyng: 'It is a mete which is lovesome and plesant to the lord.' For I saw the lord sitten as a man, and I saw neither mete ner drynke wherwith to servyn hym; this was on mervel. Another mervel was that this solemn lord had no servant but on, and hym he sent owte. I beheld, thynkyng what manner labour it myte ben that the servant shud don. And than I understode that he shuld don the gretest labor and herdest travel that is—he shuld ben a gardiner; delvyn and dykyn, swinkin and swetyn, and turne the earth upsodowne, and sekyn the depnes, and wattir the plants in tyme. And in this he shuld continu his travel and make swete flods to rennen, and noble and plenteous fruits to springen, which he shuld bryng aforn the lord and servyn hym therwith to his lykyng. And he shuld never turne agen till he had dygte this mete al redye as he knew that it lekyd the lord, and than he shuld take this mete, with the drinke in the mete, and beryn it ful worshipfully aforn the lord. And al this tyme the lord shuld sytten on the same place abydand his servant whome he sent out. And yet I merveylid from whens the servant came; for I saw in the lord that he hath wythyn hymselfe endles lif and al manner of goodnes, save that tresor that was in the erth—and that was groun[dy]d[133] in the lord in mervelous depenes of endles love—but it was not all to the worship till this servant had dygte thus nobly it, and browte it aforn him, in hymself present; and without the lord was nothing but wildernes. And I understod not all what this example ment, and therfore I merveylid whens the servant cam. In the servant is comprehendid the second person in the Trinite; and in the servant is comprehendid Adam, that is to say, al man. And therfore whan I say 'the Son', it menyth the Godhede which is even with the Fadir, and whan I sey 'the servant', it menyth Christs manhood which is rythful Adam. Be the nerehede of the servant is understode the Son, and be the stondyng on the left syde is vnderstod Adam. The lord is the Fadir, God. The servant is the Son, Christ Iesus. The Holy Gost is even love which is in them both. Whan Adam fell, God Son fell; for the rythfull onyng which was made in hevyn, God Son myte not fro Adam, for by Adam I understond all man. Adam fell fro lif to deth into the slade of this wretchid world and after that into hell. Gods Son fell with Adam into the slade of the mayden wombe, which was the fairest dauter of Adam, and therfor to excuse Adam from blame in hevyn and in erth; and mytyly he fetchid him out of hell. Be the wisdam and goodnes that was in the servant is vnderstode Godds Son. Be the por clothyng as a laborer standand nere the left syde is vnderstode the manhood and Adam, with al the mischef and febilnes tha[t][134] folowith; for in al this our good lord shewid his owne Son and Adam but one man. The vertue and the goodnes that we have is of Iesus Criste, the febilnes and the blindnes that we have is of Adam; which ii wer shewid in the servant. And thus hath our good lo[r]d[135] Iesus taken upon him al our blame; and therfore our Fadir may, ne will, no more blame assigne to us than to his owen Son, derworthy Criste. Thus was he the servant aforne his comeing into the erth, stondand redy aforne the Fader in purposs till what tyme he would send hym to don that worshipfull dede be which mankynde was browte ageyn into hevyn; that is to seyn, notwithstondyng that he is God, evyn with the Fadir as anempts the Godhede, but in his forseeing purpose that he wold be man to saven man in fulfilling of his Faders will, so he stode afore his Fader as

78

a servant, wilfully takyng upon hym al our charge. And than he stirt full redily at the Faders will, and anon he fell full low in the maydens womb, haveing no reward to himselfe ne to his herd peyns. The [wyth][136] kirtle is the flesh; the syngulhede is that there was ryte [noght][137] atwix the Godhod and manhede; the steytehede is povertye; the eld is of Adams waring; the defaceing of swete, of Adams travel; the shorthede shewith the servant labour. And thus I saw the Son stonding, sayeing in his menyng; 'Lo, my der Fader, I stond befor the in Adams kirtle al redy to sterten and to rennen. I wold ben in the erth to don thy worship whan it is thy will to send me. How long shal I desiren?' Ful sothfastly wist the Son whan it was the Fader will and how long he shal desiren; that is to sey, anempt the Godhede, for he is the wisdam of the Fader. Wherfor this mening was shewid in vnderstondyng of the manhode of Criste; for all mankynd that shal be savid be the swete incarnation and blisful passion of Criste, al is the manhood of Criste; for he is the hede and we be his members; to which members the day and the tyme is onknown whan every passand wo and sorow shal have an end, and the everlestyng ioy and bliss sha[ll][138] be fulfyled; which day and time for to se al the company of hevyn longyth. And al that shall ben under hevyn that shal come thider, ther wey is be longynge and desire; which desir and longing was shewid in the servant stondyng aforen the lord, or ell thus, in the Sons stondyng aforn the Fadir in Adams kirtle; for the langor and desire of al mankynd that shal be savid aperid in Iesus; for Iesus is al that shal be savid and al that shal be savid is Iesus; and al of the charite of God, with obediens, mekeness and patience, and vertues that longyn to us. Also in this mervelous example I have techyng with me, as it were the begynnyng of an ABC, wherby I may have sum vnderstondyng of our lo[r]dis[139] menyng; for the privities of the revelation ben hidd therin, notwithstondyng that al the shewing arn ful of privityes. The syttyng of the Fadir betokynyth his Godhede, that is to sey, for shewyng of rest and peas; for in the Godhede may be no travel. And that he shewid hymselfe as lord betokynith to our manhode. The stondyng of the servant betokynyth travel;

on syde and on the left betokynyth that he was not al worthy to stonden ever[140] ryth aforn the lord. His stertyng was the Godhede, and the rennyng was the manhede; for the Godhede sterte from the Fadir into the maydens wombe, falling into the taking of our kynde; and in this falling he toke gret sore; the sore that he toke was our flesh in which he had also swithe felyng of dedly peynis. Be that he stod dredfully aforn the lord, and not even ryth, betokynith that his clothyng was not honest to stond in eve[n][141] ryth aforn the lord; ne that myte not, ne shuld not, ben his office whil he was a laborer; ne also he myte not sitten in rest and peace with the lord till he had woon his peace rythfully with his herd travel; and be the left syde, that the Fadir left his owne Son wilfully in the manhode to suffre all mannys paynys without sparing of him. Be that his kirtle was in poynte to be raggid and rent is vnderstonden the sweppys and the scorgis, the thornys and the naylys, the drawyng and the draggyng, his tender flesh rendyng; as I saw in sum partie, the flesh was rent from the hedepanne, falland in [pecys][142] into the tyme the bledyng failyd; and than it began to dryand agen, clyngand to the bone. And be the wallowyng and wrythyng, groning and monyng, is vnderstonden that he myte never rysen al mytyly from the tyme that he was fallen into the maydens wombe till his body was slaine and ded, he yeldyng the soule in the Fadirs hands with al mankynd for whom he was sent. And at this poynte he began first to shewen his myte; for he went into helle, and whan he was there he reysid up the grit rote out of the depe depenes which rythfully was knit to hym in hey hevyn. The body was in the grave till Estern morow, and from that tyme he lay never more; for then was rythfully endid the walowyng and the wrythyng, the groning and the monyng; and our foule dedly flesh that Gods Son toke on hym, which was Adams old kirtle, steyte, bare and short, than be our saviour was made fair now,[143] white and bryte and of endles clenes, wyde and syde, fairer and richer than was than the clothyng which I saw on the Fadir; for that clothyng was blew, and Christs clothyng is now of a fair, semely medlur which is so mervelous that I can it not discrien; for it is al of very worshipps. Now sittith not the lord

on erth in wilderness, but he sittith in his noblest sete which
he made in hevyn most to his lekyng. Now stondith not the
Son aforn the Fadir as a servant dredfully, unornely clad, in
party nakid, but he stondith aforn the Fadir ever[144] rythe,
rechely clad in blissfull largess, with a corone upon his hede
of pretious richess; for it was shewid that we be his corone,
which corone is the Fadirs ioye, tho Sonys worshippe, the Holy
Gost lekyng, and endless mervelous bliss to all that be in
hevyn. Now stondith not the Son aforn the Fadir on the left
syde as a laborer, but he sittith on his Fadirs ryte hand in
endles rest and peace. But it is not ment that the Son syttith
on the ryte hond, syde be syde, as on man sittith be another
in this lif; for there is no such syttyng, as to my syte, in the
Trinite; but he sittith on his Fadirs ryte hand, that is to sey,
in the heyest noblyth of the Fadirs ioyes. Now is the spouse,
Gods Son, in peace with his lowid wife, which is the fair
mayden of endles ioye. Now sittith the Son, very God and
man, in his cety in rest and peace, which his Fadir hath adyte
to him of endles purpose; and the Fadir in the Son, and tho
Holy Gost in the Fadir and in the Son.

52

God enioyeth that he is our fadir, bother[145] *and spouse; and
how the chosen have here a medlur of wele and wo, but God
is with us in iii manner; and how we may eschew synne but
never [perfectly as in heaven]*[146]*—lii chapter.*

And thus I saw God enioyeth that he is our fader, God
enioyeth that he is our moder, and God enioyeth that he is
our very spouse, and our soule is his lovid wife. And Criste
enioyeth that he is our broder, and Iesus enioyeth that he is
our savior. Ther arn v hey ioyes, as I vnderstond, in which he
wil that we enioyen, hym praysyng, him thankyng, him loveing,
him endlesly blissand. Al that shal be savid, for the tyme of
this life, we have in us a mervelous medlur bothen of wele
and wo. We have in us our lord Iesus uprysen; we have in us

81

the wretchidnes of the mischefe of Adams fallyng, deyand. Be Criste we are stedfastly kept, and be his grace touchyng we are reysid into sekir troste of salvation. And be Adams fallyng we arn so broken in our felyng on divers manner, be synes and be sondry peynes, in which we arn made derke and so blinde that onethys we can taken ony comfort. But in our menyng we abiden God and faithfully trosten to have mercy and grace; and this is owen werkyng in us. And of his godeness he opynyth the eye of our vnderstondyng be which we have syte, sumtyme more and sumtyme less, after that God gevyth abilite to takyn. And now we arn reysid into that on, and now we are suffrid to fallen into that other. And thus is this medle so mervelous in us that onethys we knowen of our selfe or of our evyn Cristen in what way we stonden, for the merveloushede of this sundry felyng; but that ilke holy assent that we assenten to God whan we felyn hym, truly willand to be with him with al our herte with al our soule and with all our myte; and than we haten and dispisen our evil sterings and all that myte be occasion of synne gostly and bodily. And yet nevertheles whan this sweteness is hidde, we falyn ageyn into blindhede, and so into wo and tribulation on divers manner. But than is this our comfort, that we knowen in our feith that be the vertue of Criste, which is our keper, we assenten never therto, but we grutchin theragen, and duryin in peyne and wo, prayand into that tyme that he shewith him agen to us. And thus we stonden in this medlur all the dayes of our life. But he will we trosten that he is lestyngly with us, and that in iii manner: he is with us in hevyn, very man in his owne person us updrawand, and that was shewid in the gostly thrist; and he is with us in erth us ledand, and that was shewid in the thrid, wher I saw God in a poynte; and he is with us in our soule endlesly wonand, us reuland and yemand, and that was shewid in the xvith, as I shal sey. And thus in the servant was shewid the mischefe and blyndhede of Adams fallyng; and in the servant was shewid the wisdam and godeness of God Son. And in the lord was shewid the ruth and pite of Adams wo; and in the lord was shewid the hey noblyth and the endles worship that mankynde is cum to be the vertue of the passion

and the deth of his derworthy Son; and therfore mytyly he
enioyeth in his fallyng, for the hey reysing and fullhede of
bliss that mankynde is cum to, overpassing that we shuld have
had if he had not fallen; and thus to se this overpassing nobleth
was myn vnderstondyng led into God in the same tyme that
I saw the servant fallen. And thus we have now matter of
morneing, for our synne is cause of Crists paynes; and we
haive lestingly matter of ioy, for endles love made hym to
suffir. And therfore the creature that seith and felith the
werkyng of love be grace hatith nowte but synne; for of
althyng, to my syte, love and hate arn herdest and most
onmesurable contraries. And notwithstondyng all this, I saw
and understode in our lord menyng that we may not in this
life kepe us from synne as holy in ful clenes as we shal ben
in hevyn. But we may wele be grace kepe us from the synnes
which will ledyn us to endles pay[n]es,[147] as holy church techith
us, and eschewen venal, resonable upon our myte; and if we
be our blyndhede and our wretchedness ony tyme fallen, that
we redily risen, knowand the swete touching of grace, and
wilfully amenden us upon the techyng of holy chuirch after
that the synne is grevous, and gon forwith to God in love; and
neither on the on syd fallen over low, encylnand to despeyr,
ne on that other syd ben over rekles as if we gove no fors,
but nakidly knowing our feblehede, witeand that we may not
stond a twincklyng of an eye but be keping of grace, and
reverently cleven to God, on him only trostyng; for otherwise
is the beholdyng of God, and otherwise is the beholdyng of
man; for it longyth to man mekely to accusen hymselfe, and
it longith to the propir goodnes of our lord God curtesly to
excusen man. And these be ii parties that were shewid in the
double chere in which the lord beheld the fallyng of his lovid
servant. That one was shewid outward, wel mekely and myldly
with gret ruth and pite, and that of endless love. And ryth
thus will our lord that we accusen ourselfe, wilfully and sothly
seand and knowand our fallyng and all the harmes that cum
thereof, seand and witand that we may neve[r][148] restoren it,
and therwith that we wilfully and truly sen and knowen his
everlasting love that he hath[149] us, and his plenteous mercy.

And thus graciously to sen and knowen both togeder is the meke accusyng that our lord askyth of us, and hymselfe werkith it then[150] it is. And this is the lowor parte of manys life and it was shewed in the outward chere; in which shewing I saw tw[o][151] partes: that on is the reufull falling of man, that other is the worshipfull asseth that our lord hath made for man. The other cher was shewid inward, and that was mor heyly and al on; for the life and the vertue that we have in the lower parte is of the heyer, and it cummith downe to us of the kinde love of the selfe be grace. Atwixen that on and that other is ryte nowte, for it is all one love; which on blissid love hath now in us double werking; for in the lower part arn peynes and passions, ruthes and pites, mercies and forgevenes and swich other that arn profitable; but in the higer parte are none of these, but al on hey love and mervelous ioye, in which mervelous ioy all peynis are heyly restorid.[152] And in this our good lord shewid not only our excusung, but also the worshipfull nobleth that he shall bring us to, turnand al our blame into endles worshippe.

53

The kindness of God assingneth no blame to his chosen, for in these is a godly will that never consent to synne; for it behovyth the ruthfulhede so to be knitt to these that ther be a substance kept that may never be departid from hym—liii chapter.

And I saw that he will we wetyin he takith not herder the fallyng of any creatur that shall be save than he to toke the fallyng of Adam, which we knowen was endlesly lovid and sekirly kept in the tyme of all his nede, and now is blisfully restorid in hey overpassing ioyes; for our lord God is so good, so gentill and so curtes that he may never assigne defaute in whom he shall ever be blissid and praysid. And in this that I have now seyd was my desire in partie answerid, and myn gre[te][153] awer sumdele esid be the lovely, gracious shewing of our good lord; in which shewing I saw and understode ful

84

sekirly that in every soule that shal be save is a godly wille that never assent to synne, ne never shall; which wille is so good that it may never willen ylle, but eve[r]more[154] continuly it will good and werkyth good in the syte of God. Therefore our lord will we knowen it in the feith and the beleve, and namly and truly that we have all this blissid will hole and safe in our lo[r]d[155] Iesus Christe; for that ilke kind that hevyn shall be fulfillid with behoveth nedes, of Gods rythfulhede, so to be knitt and onyd to him that therin were kept a substance which myte never, ne shuld be, partid from him; and that throw his owne good will in his endles forseing purpos. And notwithstonding this rythfull knitting and this endles onyng, yet the redemption and the ageyn byeng of mankynd is nedefull and spedefull in everything, as it is don for the same entent and to the same end that holy church in our feith us techith; for I saw that God began never to loven mankynd; for ryte the same that mankynde shal ben in endles bliss fulfilland the ioye of God as anempts his werks, ryte so the same mankynd hath ben, in the forsyte of God, knowen and lovid from without begynnyng in his rytefull entent. And be the endles assent of the full accord of al the Trinite, the mid person would be ground and hede of this fair kinde, out of whom we be al cum, in whom we be all inclosid, into whome we shall all wyndyn; in him fyndyng our full hevyn in everlestand ioye be the forseing purpos of all the blissid Trinite from without begynnyng; for er that he mad us he lovid us; and whan we were made we lovid hym; and this is a love made of the kindly substantial goodnes of the Holy Gost, mytye in reson of the myte of the Fadir, and wise in mend of the wisdam of the Son; and thus is man soule made of God and in the same poynts knitt to God. And thus I vnderstond that mannys soule is made of nought, that is to sey, it is made, but of nought that is made, as thus; whan God shuld make mans body he tooke the slyppe of erth, which is a matter medlid and gaderid of all bodily things, and therof he made mannys bodye; but to the makyng of manys soule he wold take ryte nought, but made it. And thus is the kynd made rytefully onyd to the maker, which is substantial kynd onmade;

that is, God. And therefore it is that ther may, ne shall, be
ryte nowte atwix God and mannys soule. And in this endles
love mans soule is kept hole as the matter of the revelations
menyth and shewith; in which endless love we be led and kept
of God and never shall be lost; for he will we wetyn that our
soule is a lif, which lif, of his goodnes and his grace, shall lestin
in hevyn without end, him loveand, him thankand, him
praysand. And ryte the same we shall be withoute end, the
same we were tresurid in God, and hidde, knowen and lovid
from withoute begynnyng. Wherfore he will we wettyn that
the noblest thing that eve[r][156] he made is ma[n]kynd,[157] and
the fullest substance and the heyest vertue is the blissid
soule of Criste. And furthermore he will we wettyn that his
derworthy soule was preciousley knitt to him in the makeing;
which knott is sotil and so myty that is onyd into God; in which
onyng it is made endlesly holy. Furthermore, he will we wettyn
that al the soules that shall be savid in hevyn without end ar
knitt and onyd in this onyng, and made holy in this holyhede.

54

We ought to enioye that God wonyth in our soule and our soule
in God, so that atwix God and our soule is nothing, but as it
were al God; and how feith is ground of al vertue in our soule
be the Holy Gost—liiii chapter.

And for the grete endless love that God hath to al mankynde,
he makith no departing in love betwix the blissid soule of Crist
and the lest soule that shal be savid; for it is full hesy[158] to
leven and to trowen that the wonyng of the blissid soule of
Criste is full hey in the glorious Godhede, and sothly, as I
vnderstond in our lord menyng, wher the blissid soule of Crist
is, ther is the substans of al the soules that shal be savid in
Crist. Heyly owe we to enioyen that God wonyth in our soule,
and mekil more heyly owe enioyen that our soule wonyth in
God. Our soule is made to be Gods wonyng place, and the
wonyng place of the soule is God, which is onmade. And hey

vnderstondyng it is inwardly to sen and to knowen that God which is our maker wonyth in our soule; and an heyer vnderstondyng it is inwardly to sen and to knowen our soule, that is made, wonyth in Gods substance; of which substance, God, we arn that we arn. And I saw no difference atwix God and our substance, but as it were al God, and yet myn vnderstondyng toke that our substance is in God: that is to sey, that God is God, and our substance is a creture in God; for the almyty truth of the Trinite is our fader, for he made us and kepith us in him; and the depe wisdam of the Trinite is our moder in whom we arn al beclosid; the hey goodnes of the Trinite is our lord and in him we arn beclosid and he in us. We arn beclosid in the Fadir, and we arn beclosid in the Son, and we arn beclosid in the Holy Gost; and the Fader is beclosid in us, and the Son is beclosid in us, and the Holy Gost is beclosid in us: almytyhede, al wisdam, al goodnes, on God, on lord. And our feith is a vertue that comith of our kynd substance into our sensual soule be the Holy Gost, in which al our vertuys comith to us—for without that no man may receive vertue—for it is not ell but a rythe vnderstondyng with trew beleve and sekir troste of our beyng that we arn in God, and God in us, which we se not. And this vertue with al other that God hat ordeynid to us command therin, werkith in us grete things; for Crists mercifull werking is in us, and we graciosly accordand to him throw the gefts and the vertues of the Holy Gost; this werkyng makith that we arn Crists children and cristen in liveing.

55

Christ is our wey, ledand and presenting us to the Fader; and forwith as the soule is infusid in the body mercy and grace werkyn; and how the second person toke[159] our sensualite to deliver us from duble deth—lv chapter.

And thus Criste is our wey, us sekirly ledand in his lawes, and Criste in his body mytyly berith up into hevyn; for I saw that

Crist, us al havand in him that shal be savid be him, worshipfully presentith his Fader in hevyn with us; which present ful thankfully his Fader receivith and curtesly gevith to his Son, Iesus Criste; which geft and werkyng is ioye to the Fader and bliss to the Son and likyng to the Holy Gost. And of althyng that to us longith, it is most likyng to our lord that we enioyen in this ioy which is in the blisfull Trinite of our salvation. And this was sen in the ninth shewing wher it spekith more of this matter. And notwithstanding al our feling, wo or wele, God will we vnderstond and feithyn that we arn more verily in hevyin than in erth. Our feith cummith of the kynd love of our soule and of the cler lyte of our reson and of the stedfast mend which we have of God in our first makyng. And what tyme that our soule is inspirid into our body, in which we arn made sensual, also swithe mercy and grace begynyth to werkyng, haveing of us cure and kepyng with pite and love; in which werkyng the Holy Gost formyth in our feith hope that we shal cum agen up aboven to our substance, into the vertue of Criste, incresid and fulfillid throw the Holy Gost. Thus I vnderstond that the sensualite is groundid in kind, in mercy, and in grace; which ground abylith us to receive gefts that leden us to endles life; for I saw full sekirly that our substance is in God, and also I saw that in our sensualite God is; for the selfe poynte that our soule is mad sensual, in the selfe poynt is the cite of God, ordeynid to him from withouten begynnyng; in which se he commith and never shal remove it, for God is never out of the soule in which he wonen blisfully without end. And this was sen in the xvi shewing wer it seith: 'The place that Iesus takith in our soule he shal never remov it.' And all the gefts that God may geve to cretures he hath geven to his Son Iesus for us; which gefts he, wonand in us, hath beclosid in him into the time that we be waxen and growne, our soule with our body and our body with our soule, neyther of hem takeing help of other, till we be browte up into stature as kynd werkyth; and than, in the ground of kind with werkyng of mercy, the Holy Gost graciously inspirith into us gifts ledand to endless life. And thus was my vnderstondyng led of God to sen in him and to vnderstonden, to weten and

88

to knowen, that our soule is made trinite, like to the onmade blisfull Trinite, knowen and lovid fro without begynnyng; and in the making vnyd to the maker as it is afornseid. This syte was full swete and mervelous to beholden, pesible and restfull, sekir and delectabil. And for the worshipfull onyng that was thus made of God betwix the soule and body, it behovith needs to ben that mankynd shal be restorid from duble deth; which restoring might neve[r][160] be into the time that the second person in the Trinite had takyn the lower party of mankynde, to whom the heyest was onyd in the first makyng; and these ii partes were in Criste, the heyer and the lower, which is but on soule. The heyer part was on in peace with God in full ioy and bliss; the lower partie, which is sensualite, suffrid for the salvation of mankynd. And these ii partes were seene and felt in the viii shewing, in which my body was fulfillid of feling and mynd of Crists passion and his deth. And ferthermore, with this was a sotil feling and privy inward syte of the hey parte that I was shewid in the same tyme, wher I myte not, for the mene profir, lokyn up onto hevyn; and that was for that mytye beholdyng of the inward lif; which inward lif is that hey substance, that pretious soule, which is endlesly enioyand in the Godhede.

56

It is esier to know God than our soule, for God is to us nerer than that, and therfore if we will have knowing of it we must seke into God; and he will we desir to have knowledge of kynde mercy and grace—lvi chapter.

And thuss I saw full sekirly that it is ridier to us to cum to the knowyng of God than to knowen our owne soule; for our soule is so deepe groundid in God, and so endlesly tresorid, that we may not cum to the knowing therof till we have first knowing of God, which is the maker to whom it is onyd. But notwith-stondyng, I saw that we have of fulhede to desiren wisely and treuly to knowen our owne soule, wherby we are lernid to

sekyn it wher it is, and that is in God. And thus be gracious
ledyng of the Holy Gost we should knowen hem both in on,
whither we be sterid to knowen God or our soule; they arn
both good and trew. God is nerer to us than our owen soule;
for he is ground in whom our soule stondith and he is mene
that kepith the substance and the sensualite to God[161] so that
thai shall never departyn; for our soule sittith in God in very
rest and our soule stondith in God in very strength and our
soule is kindly rotid in God in endles love. And therfore if
we wil have knowlidge of our soule and comenyng and
daliance therwith, it behovith to sekyn into our lord God in
whom it is inclosid. And of this inclos I saw and understode
more in the xvi shewing, as I shall sey. And anempts our
substan[c]e[162] and sensualite, it may rytely be clepid our soule;
and that is be the onyng that it hath in God. The worshipfull
cyte that our lord Iesus sittith in, it is our sensualite in which
he is inclosid; and our kindly substance is beclosid in Iesus
with the blissid soule of Criste sitting in rest in the Godhede.
And I saw full sekirly that it behovith neds to be that we shuld
ben in longyng and in penance into the time that we be led
so depe into God that we verily and trewly knowen our own
soule. And sothly I saw that into this hey depenes our good
lord himselfe ledith us in the same love that he made us, and
in the same love that he bowte us be mercy and grace throw
vertue of his blissid passion. And notwithstondyng al this, we
may never come to full knowyng of God till we know first
clerely our own soule; for into the tyme that it is in the full
myts we may not be al ful holy; and that is that our sensualite
be the vertue of Crists passion be browte up to the substan[c]e,[163] with al the profitts of our tribulation that our lord
shall make us to gettyn be mercy and grace. I had in partie
touching, and it is grounded in kynde; that is to sey, our reson
is groundid in God which is substantial heyhede.[164] Of this
substantial kindhede mercy and grace springith and spredith
into us, werking al things in fulfilling of our ioy. These arn
our grounds in which we have our incres and our fulfilling;
for in kind we have our life and our beyng, and in mercy and
grace we have our incres and our fulfilling; these be iii

90

propertes in on goodnes, and wher on werkith all werkyn in the things which be now longyng to us. God will we onderstond, desirand of al our hert and al our strength to have knoing of hem more and mor into the time that we ben fulfillid; for fully to knowen hem and clerely to sen hem is not ell but endless ioy and bliss that we shall have in hevyn; which God will they ben begun here in knowing of his love; for only be our reson we may not profitteyn, but if we have verily therwith mynd and love; ne only in our kindly ground that we have in God we may not be savid, but if we have connyng of the same ground, mercy and grace; for of these iii we[r]kyng[165] altogeder we receive all our goodnes; of the which the first arn goods of kynd; for in our first makyng God gaf us as ful goods and also greter godes as we myte receivin only in our spirite, but his forseing purpos in his endles wisdam wold that we wern duble.

57

In our subs[t]ance[166] we aren full, in our sensualite we faylyn, which God will restore be mercy and grace; and how our kinde which is the heyer part is knitt to God in the makyng, and God, Iesus, is knitt to our kind in the lower part in our flesh takyng; and of feith spryngyn other vertues; and Mary is our moder— lvii chapter.

And anempts our substance, he made us nobil and so rich that evermore we werkyn his will and his worship. There [I][167] say 'we', it menith man that shall be savid; for sothly I saw that we arn that he lovith and don that he lekyth lestingly withouten ony styntyng; and of the gret riches and of the hey noble, vertues be mesur come to our soule what tyme it is knitt to our body; in which knitting we arn made sensual. And thus in our substance we arn full, and in our sensualite we faylyn; which faylyng God will restore and fulfill be werkyng mercy and grace plentiously flowand into us of his owne kynd godhede. And thus his kinde godehede makith that mercy and

grace werkyn in us; and the kind godhede that we have of him
abilith us to receive the werking of mercy and grace. I saw
that our kind is in God hole, in which he makyth diverssetis
flowand out of him to werkyn his will, whom kind kepith, and
mercy and grace restorith and fulfillith; and of these non shall
perishen; for our kind which is the heyer part is knitt to God
in the makyng; and God is knitt to our kinde which is the
lower partie in our flesh takyng; and thus in Christ our ii kinds
are onyd; for the Trinite is comprehendid [in][168] Criste in
whome our heyer partie is groundid and rotid, and our lower
partie the second person hath taken, which kynd first to him
was adyte; for I saw ful sekirly that all the workes that God
hath done, or ever shall, wer ful knowen to him and afornseen
from without begynning; and for love he made mankynd and
for the same love himself wold be man. The next good that
we receive is our feith in which our profittyng begynnyth; and
it commith of the hey riches of our kinde substance into our
sensual soule; and it is groundid in us and we in that throw
the kynde goodness of God be the werkyng of mercy and
grace. And therof commen al othir goods be which we arn led
and savid; for the commandements of God commen therein
in which we owe to have ii manner of vnderstondyng which
are: his bidding to love them and to kepyn; that other is that
we owe to knowen his forbyddings, to haten and to refusen;
for in these ii is all our werkyn comprehendid. Also in our
feith commen the seven sacraments ech folowing other in
order as God hath ordeyned hem to us, and al manner of
vertues; for the same vertues that we have receivid of our
substance, gevyn to us in kinde, be the goodness of God the
same vertues, be the werkyng of mercy, arn geven to us in
grace, throw the Holy Gost renued; which vertues and gyfts
are tresurd to us in Iesus Christ; for in that ilk tyme that God
knitted him to our body in the maydens womb he toke our
sensual soule; in which takyng, he us al haveyng beclosid in
him, he onyd it to our substance, in which onyng he was perfect
man; for Criste havyng knitt in him ilk man that shall be savid,
is perfit man. Thus our lady is our moder in whome we are
all beclosid and of hir borne in Christe; for she that is moder

of our savior is moder of all that shall be savid in our savior.
And our savior is our very moder in whom we be endlesly
borne and neve[r][169] shall come out of him. Plenteously and
fully and swetely was this shewid; and it is spoken of in the
first wher he seith we arn all in him beclosid and he is beclosid
in us; and that is spoken of in the xvi shewing wher it seith
he sittith in our soule; for it is his likeyng to reygne in our
vnderstondyng blisfully, and sitten in our soule restfully, and
to wonen in our soule endlesly, us al werkeng into hym; in
which werkyng he will we ben his helpers, gevyng to him al
our entendyng, lerand his loris, kep[yng][170] his lawes, desirand
that al be done that he doith, truely trosting in hym; for sothly
I saw that our substan[c]e[171] is in God.

58

*God was never displesid with his chosin wif; and of iii properties
in the Trinite: faderhede, moderhede and lordhede; and how
our substance is in every person, but our sensualite is in Criste
alone—lviii chapter.*

God, the blisful Trinite which is everlestand beyng, ryte as he
is endless from without begynnyng, ryte so it was in his
purpose endles to maken mankynd; which fair kynd first was
adyte to his owen Son, the second person. And whan he wold,
be full accord of all the Trinite, he made us all at onys; and
in our makyng he knitt us and onyd us to hymse[l]fe;[172] be
which onyng we arn kept as clene and as noble as we were
made. Be the vertue of the ilke pretious onyng we loven our
maker and liken him, praysen him and thankyng him and
endlesly enioyen in him. And this is the werke which is
wrought continuly in every soule that shal be save; which is
the godly will aforanseid. And thus in our makeyng God
almigty is our kindely fader; and God al wisdam is our kindly
moder, with the love and the goodnes of the Holy Gost; which
is al one God, on lord. And in the knittyng and in the onyng
he is our very trew spouse, and we his lovid wif and his fair

maiden, with which wif he is never displesid; for he seith: 'I love the and thou lovist me, and our love shal never be departid on to.' I beheld the werkyng of all the blissid Trinite, in which beholdyng I saw and vnderstode these iii properties: the properte of the faderhede, the properte of the moderhede and the properte of the lordhede in one God. In our Fader almyty we have our keping and our bliss as anemts our kind[l]y[173] substance, which is to us be our makyng without begynnyng;[174] and in the second person, in witt and wisdam, we have our keping as anempts our sensualite, our restoryng and our savyng; for he is our moder, brother and savior. And in our good lord the Holy Gost we have our rewarding and our [y]eldyng[175] for our lifyng and our travel; and endless overpassing all that we desiren, in his mervelous curtesy, of his hey plentivous grace. For al our life is in thre. In the first we have our beyng and in the second we have our encresyng and in the thrid we hav our fulfilling. The first is kinde; the second is mercy; the thred is grace. For the first: I saw and vnderstod that the hey myte of the Trinite is our fader, and the depe wisdam of the Trinite is our moder, and the grete love of the Trinite is our lord; and al this have we in kynd and in our substantial makyng. And ferthermore, I saw that the second person, which is our moder substantial, that same derworthy person is become our moder sensual; for we arn duble of Gods making: that is to say, substantiall and sensual. Our substance is the heyer parte, which we have in our fader, God almyty; and the second person of the Trinite is our moder in kynde in our substantiall makeyng, in whome we arn groundid and rotid, and he is our moder in mercy in our sensualite takyng. And thus our moder is to us dyvers manner werkyng, in whom our parties are kepid ondepartid; for in our moder, Criste, we profitten and encresin, and in mercy he reformith us and restorith, and, be the vertue of his passion and his deth and uprisyng, onyth us to our substance. Thus werkith our moder in mercy to all his children which arn to him buxum and obedient. And grace werkyth with mercy, and namely in ii propertes as it was shewid; which werkyng longyth to the tred person, the Holy Gost. He werkith rewardyng and

gefyng; rewardyng is a large gevyng of trewth that the lord
doth to hym that hath travellid, and gevyng is a curtes workyng
which he doith frely of grace fulfill, and overpassand al that
is deservid of cretures. Thus in our fader, God almigty, we
have our beyng; and in our moder of mercy we have our
reformyng and restoryng, in whome our partes are onyd and
all made perfitt man; and be yeldyng and [gevyng][176] in grace
of the Holy Gost we arn fulfilled. And our substance is our
fader, God almyty, and our substance is ou[r][177] moder, God
al wisdamm, and our substance is in our lord the Holy Gost,
God al goodnes; for our substance is hole in ilke person of
the Trinite, which is on God. And our sensualite is only in the
second person, Crist Iesus, in whom is the Fader and the Holy
Gost; and in him and be him we arn mytyly taken out of helle
and out of the wretchidnes in erth, and worshipfully browte
up into hevyn and blisfully onyd to our substance, incresid in
riches and noblith, be al the vertue of Criste and be the grace
and werkyng of the Holy Gost.

59

Wickednes is turnyd to bliss be mercy and grace in the
chosyn, for the properte of God is to do good ageyn ille, be
Iesus our moder in kynd grace; and the heyest soule in
vertue is mekest, of which ground we have other vertues—lix
chapter.

And all this bliss we have be mercy and grace; which manner
of bliss we myte never had ne knowen but if that propertes
of goodness which is God had ben contraried, wherby we have
this bliss; for wickednes hath ben suffrid to rysen contrarye to
the goodnes, and the goodnes of mercy and grace contraried
ageyn the wickidnes, and turnyd al to goodness and to worship
to al these that shal be savid; for it is the properte in God
which doith good agen evil. Thus Iesus Criste that doith good
agen evill is our very moder; we have our beyng of him wher
the ground of moderhed begynnyth, with al the swete kepyng

95

of love that endlessly folowith. As veryly as God is our fader, as verily God is our moder; and that shewid he in all, and namely in these swete words where he seith 'I it am', that is to seyen: 'I it am: the myte and the goodness of the faderhed. I is am: the wisdam of the moderhede. I it am: the lyte and the grace that is al blissid love. I it am: the Trinite. I it am: the unite. I am the sovereyne goodness of all manner of thyngs. I am that makyth the to loven. I am that makyth the to longen. I it am: the endles fulfilling of al trew desires.' For then the soule is heyest, noblest and worthyest when it is lowest, mekest and myldhest; and of this substantial ground we have al our vertues and our sensualite be gyft of kynd and be helpyng and spedyng of mercy and grace, without the which we may not profitten. Our hey fader, God almyty, which is beyng, he knew us and lovid us fro aforn any tyme; of which knoweing, in his mervelous depe charite be the forseing endless councel of all the blissid Trinite, he wold that the second person shuld becom our moder, our brother and our savior. Wherof it folowith that as verily as God is our fader, as verily God is our moder. Our fader [wyllyth],[178] our moder werkyth, our good lord the Holy Gost confirmith. And therfore it longyth to us to loven our God in whom we have our being, him reverently thankyng and praiseyng of our makyng, mytily prayeng to our moder of mercy and pite, and to our lord the Holy Gost of helpe and grace; for in these iii is all our life—kynde, mercy and grace; whereof we have mekehede, myldhede, patiens and pite, and hatyng of synne and wickidnes; for it longith properly to vertues to haten synne and wickidness. And thus is Iesus our very moder in kynde, of our first makyng, and he is our very moder in grace be takyng of our kynde made. All the fair werkyng and all the swete kindly office of dereworthy moderhede is impropried to the second person; for in him we have this godly will hole and save withoute ende, both in kinde and grace, of his owne proper goodnes. I vnderstode iii manner of beholdyng of moderhede in God: the first is groundid of our kinde makeying; the second is taken of our kinde, and there begynnyth the moderhede of grace; the thrid is moderhede of werkyng, and therein is a forth-spreadyng, be the same grace, of length and bredth and of heyth and of depenes withouten end, and al his own luf.

60

How we be bowte ageyn and forthspred be mercy and grace of our swete, kynde and ever lovyng moder Iesus, and of the propertes of moderhede; but Iesus is our very moder, not fedyng us with mylke but with himselfe, opening his syde onto us and chalengyng al our love—lx chapter.

But now behovyth to sey a litil mor of this forthspredyng, as I vnderstond in the menyng of our lord, how that we be bowte agen be the moderhede of mercy and grace into our kyndly stede wher that we were made by the moderhede of kynd love; which kynd love it never levyth us. Our kynd moder, our gracious moder, for he wold al holy become our moder in althyng, he toke the ground of his werke full low and ful myldely in the maydens womb. And that he shewid in the first, where he browte that meke mayde aforn the eye of myn vnderstondyng in the simple statur as she was whan she conceivid; that is to sey, our hey God is sovereyn wisdom of all, in this low place he raysid him and dyte him ful redy in our pore flesh, himselfe to don the service and the office of moderhede in allthyng. The moders service is nerest, redyest and sekirest,[179] for it is most of trueth. This office ne myte, ne couthe, ne never non don to the full [but][180] he alone. We wetyn that all our moders beryng is us to peyne and to deyeng; and what is that but our very moder Iesus, he, al love, beryth us to ioye and to endles lyving; blissid mot he be! Thus he susteynith us within himselfe in love, and traveled into the full tyme that he wold suffre the sharpist throwes and the grevousest peynes that ever were or ever shall be, and dyed at the last. And whan he had don, and so born us to bliss, yet myte not al this makyn aseth to his mervelous love; and that shewid he in these hey overpassing wordes of love: 'If I myte suffre more, I wold suffre more.' He myte ne more dyen, but

he wold not stynten of werkyng. Wherfore than him behovyth
to fedyn us, for the dereworthy love of moderhede hath made
him dettor to us. The moder may geven hir child soken her
mylke, but our pretious moder Iesus, he may fedyn us with
himselfe; and doith full curtesly and full tenderly with the
blissid sacrament that is pretious fode of very lif. And with al
the swete sacraments he susteynith us ful mercifully and
graciously. And so ment he in this blissid word wher that he
seid 'I it am that holy church prechith the and techith the';
that is to sey: 'All the helth and lif of sacraments, al the vertue
and grace of my word, all the godness that is ordeynid in holy
church for the, I it am.' The moder may leyn the child tenderly
to her brest, but our tender moder Iesus, he may homley leden
us into his blissid brest be his swete open syde, and shewyn
therin party of the Godhede and the ioyes of hevyn, with gostly
sekirnes of endless bliss; and that shewid in the [x],[181] gevyng
the same vnderstondyng in this swete word wher he seith 'Lo,
how I love the', beholdand into his syde, enioyand. This fair
lovely word 'moder', it is so swete and so kynd of the self that
it may ne verily be seid of none but of him, and to hir that is
very moder of hym and of all. To the properte of moderhede
longyth kinde love, wisdam and knowing, and it is good; for
thow it be so that our bodily forthbrynging be but litil, low
and semple in regard of our gostly forthbringing, yet it is he
that doth it in the creatures be whom that it is done. The
kynde, loveand moder that wote and knowith the nede of hir
child, she kepith it ful tenderly as the kind and condition of
moderhede will. And as it wexith in age she chongith hir
werking but not hir love. And whan it is waxen of more age,
she suffrid that it be bristinid in brekyng downe of vices to
makyn the child to receivyn vertues and graces. This werkyng,
with al that be fair and good, our lord doith it in hem be whom
it is done. Thus he is our moder in kynde be the werkyng of
grace in the lower parte, for love of the heyer parte. And he
will that we know it; for he will have al our love festynyd to
him. And in this I saw that all our dett that we owen, be Gods
biddyng, be faderhede and moderhede, for Gods faderhede
and moderhede is fulfillid in trew lovyng of God; which blissid

98

love Christ werkyth in us. And this was shewid in all, and namly in the hey plentivous words wher he seith: 'I it am that thou lovest.'

61

Iesus usith more tenderness in our gostly bringing forth; thow he suffrith us to fallyn in knowing of our wretchidness, he hastily reysith us, not brekyng his love for our trespass, for he may not suffre his child to perish; for he will that we have the properte of a child, fleing to him alway in our necessite—lxi chapter.

And in our gostly forthbringyng he usith mor tenderness of keping, without ony likenes, be as mech as our soule is of more price in his syte. He ky[n]delyth[182] our vnderstondyng, he directith our weys, he esith our consciens, he comfortith our soule, he lightith our our herte and gevith us, in parte, knowyng and lovyng in his blisful Godhede, with gracious mynd in his swete manhede and his blissid passion, with curtes mervelyng in his hey, overpassyng goodnes; and makith us to loven al that he loveth for his love, and to bend payd with him and all his werkes. And we fallen, hastily he reysith us be his lovely clepyng and gracious touchyng. And whan we be thus st[r]engtid[183] be his swete werkyng, than we wilfully chesyn him, be his swete grace, to be his servants and his lovers lestingly without end. And after this he suffrith sum of us to fallen more hard and more grevously than ever we diden afore, as us thynkyth. And than wene we that be not al wyse that al were nowte that we have begun. But it is no so; for it nedith us to fallen, and it nedith us to sen it; for if we felle nowte we should not knowen how febil and how wretchid we arn of ourselfe; ne also we shuld not fulsomely so knowen the mervelous love of our maker; for we shal sen verily in hevyn withouten end that we have grevously synned in this life, and notwithstondyng this, we shal sen that we were never hurt in his love, ne were never the less of price in his syte. And be

99

the assay of this failyng we shall have an hey, mervelous knoweing of love in God without end; for herd and mervelous is that love which may nowte, ne will not, be brokin for trespas. And this is one vnderstonding of profite. Another is the lownes and mekenes that we shal gettyn be the syte of our fallyng; for therby we shal heyly ben raysid in hevyn; to which reysing we might never a come withoute that mekeness. And therfore it nedyth us to sen it, and if we sen it not, thow we fellyn, it shuld not profitt us. And commenly, first we fallen, and syth we sen it; and both of the mercy of God. The moder may suffre the child to fallen sumtyme and be disesid in dyvers manners for the owen profitt, but she may neve[r][184] suffre that ony maner of peril cum to the child, for love. And thow our erthly moder may suffre hir child to perishen, our hevynly moder Iesus may not suffre us that arn his children to perishen; for he is almyty, all wisdom and al love; and so is non but he. Blissid mot he ben! But oftentymes whan our fallyn and our wretchidnes is shewid us, we arn so sore adred and so gretly ashamid of ourselfe that onethys we wettyn where that we may holden us. But than will not our curtes moder that we fle awey, for him wer nothing lother. But he will than that we usen the condition of a child; for whan it is disesid or dred it rennith hastely to the moder for helpe with al the myte; so wil he that we don as a meke child, seyand thus: 'My kind moder, my gracious moder, my dereworthy moder, have mercy on me. I have made myselfe foule and onlike to the, and I ne may ne can amenden it but with prive helpe and grace.' And if we fele us not than esyd al swithe, be we sekir that he usith the condition of a wise moder; for if he sen that it be more profitt to us to morne and to wepen, he suffrith it with ruth and pite into the best tyme, for love. And he will than that we usen the propertie of a child that evermor kindly trosteth to the love of the moder in wele and in wo. And he will that we taken us mytyly to the feith of holy church and fyndyn there our dereworthy moder in solace of trew vnderstondyng with al the blissid common; for on singler person may oftentymes be broken as it semyth to selfe, but the hole body of holy church was never broken, ne never shall, withouten end. And therfore a sekir thing it is, a good and a gracious, to willen mekely and mytyly ben susteynd and onyd to our moder, holy church, that is Crist Iesus; for the foode[185] of mercy that is his dereworthy blood and pretious water is plentious to make us faire and clene. The blissid wound of our savior ben open and enioyen to helyn us; the swete gracious hands of our moder be redy and diligently aboute us; for he in al this werkyng usith the office of a kinde nurse and hath not all to don but to entendyn abouten the salvation of hir child. It is his office to saven us, it is his worship to don us,[186] and it is his will we knowen it; for he will we loven him swetely and trosten in him mekely and mytyly. And this shewid he in these gracious words: 'I kepe the ful sekirly.'

62

The love of God suffrith never his chosen to lose tyme, for all their troble is turnyd into endles ioye; and how we arn al bownden to God for kindness and for grace; for every kind is in man and us nedyth not to seke out to know sondry kindes, but to holy church—lxii chapter.

For in that tyme he shewid our frelte and our fallyngs, our brekyngs and our nowtyngs, our dispits and our outcastings: all our wo so ferforth as methowte it my[ght][187] fallen in this life. And therwith he shewid his blissid myte, his blissid wisdam, his blissid love, that he kepyth us in this tyme as tenderly and as swetely to his worship and as sekirly to our salvation as he doith whan we are in most solace and comfort; and therto he reysith us gostly and heyly in hevyn, and turnith it al to his worship and to our ioye, withoute end; for his love suffrith us never to lose tyme. And all this is of the kind goodnes of God be the werkyng of grace. God is kynde in his being: that is to sey, that goodnes that is kind, it is God. He is the ground, he is the substance, he is the same thing that is kindhede, and he is very fader and very moder of kynde. And all kindes that he hath made to flowen out of him to werkyn his will, it shall be restorid and browte ageyn into him be the salvation of man throw the werking of grace; for of all kyndes that he hath set in dyvers creatures be parte, in man is all the hole in fulhede, in vertue, in fairhede and in goodhede, in rialtie and nobley, in al manner of solemnite of pretioushede and worshipp. Here may we sen that we arn al bound to God for kinde, and we arn al bound to God for grace. Here may we sen us nedith not gretly to seken fer out to knowen sundry kindes, but to holy church, into our moder brest; that is to sey, into our owen soule, wher our lord wonnyth. And ther shall we fynde all; now, in feith and in vnderstondyng; and after, verily in himselfe, clerely, in bliss. But no man ne woman take this singler to himselfe; for it is not so, it is general; for it is our pretious Criste and to him was this fair kind dyte, for the worship and noblyth of mannys makyng, and for the ioye and the bliss of mannys salvation; ryte as he saw, wiste and knew from without begynni[n]g.[188]

63

Synne is more peynfull than hell, and vile and hurting kinde, but grace savith kinde and destroyith synne; the children of Iesus be not yet all borne, which pass not the stature of childhood, livyng in febilness till thei come to hevyn wher ioyes arn ever new begynnand without end—lxiii chapter.

Here we may sen that we have verily of kinde to haten synne, and we have verily of grace to haten synne; for kinde is al good and faire in the selfe, and grace was sent out to saven kind and destroyen synne and b[r]yngen[189] ageyn fair kinde to the blissid poynt fro whens it came, that is God, with mor noble and worshipp be the vertuous werkeyng of grace; for it shal be sen afor God of al his holy in ioye without end that kind hath ben assayed in the fire of tribulation and therin founden no lak, no defaut. Thus is kind and grace of an accord; for grace is God as kind is God. He is ii in manner werkyng and one in love, and neyther of hem werkyth without the

other, non be departid. And whan we be mercy of God and
with his helpe accorden us to kynde and grace, we shall seen
verily that synne is very viler and peynfuller than helle,
without likenes; for it is contrarious to our fair kinde; for as
sothly as synne is onclene, as soth[l]y[190] is it onkinde, and thus
an horrible thing to sen to the lovid soule that wold be al faire
and shynand in the syte of God as kinde and grace te[c]hith.[191]
But be we not adred of this, but in as much as drede may
spede us, but mekely make we our mone to our dereworthy
moder, and he shal al besprinkle us in his precious blode and
make our soule ful soft and ful myld, and hele us ful faire be
proces of tyme, ryte as it is most worship to him and ioy to
us without end. And of this swete fair werkyng he shall
neve[r][192] cesyn ne stintin till all his derworthy children be
born and forth browte. And that shewid he wher he shewid
vnderstonding of gostly threst, that is the lovelongyng that
shal lestin till domysday. Thus in very moder, Iesus, our life
is groundid in the forseing wisdam of himselfe from without
begynnyng, with the hey myte of the Fader and the hey
sovereyn goodnes of the Holy Gost. And in the takyng of our
kinde he quicknid us, in his blissid deying upon the cross he
bare us to endless life; and fro that time, and now, and ever
shall onto domysday, he fedith us and [fordreth][193] us; and
ryte as that hey sovereign kindness of moderhede[194] and as
kindly nede of childhede askith. Faire and swete is our hevenly
moder in the syte of our soule; precious and lovely arn the
gracious children in the syte of our hevinly moder, with
myldhede and mekeness and all the fair vertues that long to
children in kynde; for kindly the child dispeirith not of the
moder love; kindly the child presumith not of the selfe; kindly
the child lovith the moder and ilke on of the othe[r];[195] these
arn the fair vertues, with all other that ben like, wherwith our
hevenly moder is servid and plesyd. And I vnderstode non
heyer stature in this life than childhode, in febilness and
fayleing of myte and of witte, into the time that our gracious
moder hath browte us up to our faders bliss. And than shall
it verily be made knowen to us his menyng in these swete
words wher he seith: 'Al shall be wele; and thou shalt sen

thyselfe that al maner thyng shal ben wele.'[196] And than shall the bliss of our moder in Criste be new to begynnen in the ioyes of our God; which new begynning shal lesten without end, new begynnand. Thus I vnderstode that al his blissid children which ben comen out of him be kinde shal be bowte ageyn into him be grace.

64

The xv revelation is as it shewid etc.; the absense of God in this life is our ful gret peyne, besyde other travels, but we shal sodenly be taken fro all peyne, having Iesus to our moder; and our patient abyding is gretly plesyng to God, and God wil take our disese lightly, for love, thinkand us alwey at the poynte to be deliverid—lxiiii chapter.

Aforn this tyme I had gret longyng and desire of Goddis gifte to be deliverid of this world and of this lif; for oftentimes I beheld the wo that is here, and the wele and the bliss that is beyng there. And if ther had ben no peyn in this lif but the absens of our lord, methowte it was sumtime mor than I myte baren; and this made me to morn and besyly to longen, and also of myn owen wretchidnes, slawth and wekehede, that me lekid not leveyn and to travelyn as me fel to don. And to all this our curtes lord answerid for comfort and patiens, and said these words: 'Sodenly thou shal be taken fro al thy peyne, fro al thi sekeness, fro al this disese and fro al the wo. And thou shalt commen up aboven, and thou shalt have me to thi mede, and thou shal be fulfillid of love and of bliss. And thou shal never have no maner of peyne,[197] no manner of mislekyn no wanting of will, but ever ioye and bliss withouten ende. What shuld it than agrevyn the to suffre awhile, sen that it is my will and my worship?' And in this word, 'Sodenly thou shal be taken', I saw that God rewardith man of the patiens that he hath in abyding Gods will, and of his tyme, and that man length his patiens over the tyme of his living; for onknowing of his tyme of passing, that is a gret profitt; for if a man knew his time, he shuld not have patience over that tyme. And as God will while the soule is in the body it semyt to the selfe that it is ever at the poynte to be takyn; for al this life and this langor that we have here is but a poynte, and whan we arn taken sodenly out of peyn into bliss, than peyn shall be nowte. And in this tyme I saw a body lyand on the erth, which body shewid hevy and ogyley, withoute shappe and forme as it were a bolned quave of styngand myre. And sodenly out of this body sprang a ful fair creature, a little childe full shapen and formid, swifie[198] and lively, whiter than lilly, which sharpely glode up onto hevyn. And the bolnehede of the body betokenith gret wretchidnes of our dedly flesh, and the littlehede of the child betokenith the clenes of purity in the soule. And [I][199] thowte: 'With this body belevith[200] no fairehede of this child, no on this child dwellith no foulehede of this body.' It is ful blisfull, man to be taken fro peyne, mor than peyne to be taken fro man; for if peyn be taken fro us it may commen agen. Therfore it is a severen comfort and blissfull beholdyng in a lovand soule [that][201] we shal be taken fro peyne; for in this behest I saw a mervelous[202] compassion that our lord hath in us for our wo, and a curtes behoting of clene deliverance; for he will that we be comforted in the overpassing; and that he shewid in these words: 'And thou shalt come up aboven; and thou shal have me to thi mede; and thou shall be fullfillid of ioye and bliss.' It is God will that we setten the poynte of our thowte in this blisfull beholdyng as often as we may, and as long tyme kepen us therin with his grace; for this is a blissid contemplation to the soule that is led of God, and full mekil to his worship for the time that it lestith. And we falyn ageyn to our hevynes and gostly blyndhede and felyng of peyens gostly and bodily be our frelte, it is God will that we knowen that he hath not forgetten us. And so menith he in thes words and seith for comfort: 'And thou shall never more have peyne, no manner sekenes, no maner mislekyng, non wanting of will, but over[203] ioy and bliss withouten ende. What shuld it than agrevyn the to suffre awhile seing it is my will and my worshippe?' It is God will we taken his behests and his comfortings as largely and as

mytyly as we may taken hem. And also he will that we taken
our abiding and our diseses as lytely as we may taken hem,
and set hem at nowte; for the lyter we taken hem and the less
price we setten at hem for love, the less peyne shall we have
in the feling of hem, and the more thanke and mede shal we
have for hem.

65

He that chesith God for love, with reverent mekeness, is sekir
to be savid; which reverent mekenes seith the lord mervelous
grete, and the selfe mervelous litil; and it is God will we drede
nothing but him, for the power of our enemy is taken in our
freinds hand; and therfore al that God doith shall be gret likyng
to us—lxv chapter.

And thus I vnderstode that what man or woman wilfully
chesith God in this life for love, he may be sekir that he is
lovid without end; which endless love werkith in him that
grace; for he will that we kepe this trosty, that we be all sekir
in hope of the bliss of hevyn whil we arn here, as we shall be
in sekirnes whan we arn there. And ever the more likyng and
ioy that we taken in this sekirness with reverens and mekenes,
the better likyth him, as it was shewid. This reverens that I
mene is a holy, curtes drede of our lord, to which mekeness
is knitt: and that is, that a creture seith the lord mervelous
grete, and the selfe mervelous litil; for these vertues arn had
endlesly to the lovid of God, and it mon now ben sen and felt
in mesure be the gracious presence of our lord whan it is;
which presens in althing is most desirid, for it werkith
mervelous sekirness, in trew feith and sekir hope be gretness
of charite, in drede that is swete and delectable. It is God will
that I se myselfe as mekil bounden to him in love as if he had
don for me al that he hath don. And thus should every soule
thinkyn innward of his lover: that is to seyn, the charite of
God makyth in us such a unite that whan it is trewly seen no
man can parten himse[l]fe[204] fro other. And thus oweth our

106

soule to thinken that God hath don for him al that he hath don; and this shewith he to maken us to loven him and nowte drede but him; for it is his will that we wetyn that al the myte of our enemy is token into our frends hand; and therfore the soule that wott sekirly this, he shall not dredyn but him that he lovith. All our dreds he setteth among passions and bodely sekenes and imaginations, and therfore thow we be in so mech peyne, wo and disese that us thinkith we can thynke ryte nowte but that we arn in, or that we felyn, as sone as we may, pass we lytely over and sett we it at nowte. And why? For God will we knowen, if [we]²⁰⁵ knowen him and loven him and reverently dredyn him, we shall have peas and ben in grete rest; and it shall be gre[at]²⁰⁶ lykyng to us all that he doith. And this shewid our lord in these words: 'What shuld it than agrevyn the to suffre awhile, sith it is my will and my worshippe?' Now have I told you of xv revelations as God vouchsafe to ministren hem to mynd, renewid by lyghtings and tuchyngs, I hope, of the same spirite that shewid hem all; of which xv sheweings the first beganne erly on the morne, aboute the howre of fowre, and it lestid, shewing be proccess ful faire and sekirly, ich folowand other, till it was none of the day overpassid.

66

The xvi revelation etc., and it is conclusion and confirmation to all xv; and of hir frelte and morning in disese and lyte speking after the gret comfort of Iesus, seying she had ravid, which, being hir gret sekeness, I suppose was but venial synne; but yet the devil after that had gret power to vexin hir ner to deth—lxvi chapter.

And after this the good lord shewid the xvi on the night folowing, as I shall seyn after; which xvi was conclusion and confirmation to all xv. But first me behovith to tellen you as anempt my febilnes, wretchidnes and blindness. I have seid in the begynning 'And in this al my peine was sodenly taken

from me'; of which peyne I had no grefe, no disese, as long
as the xv shewings lestid folowand; and at the end al was close
and I saw no more. And sone I felt that I shuld liven and
langiren; and anon my sekenes cam agen: first in my hede,
with a sound and a dynne; and sodenly all my body was
fu[1]fillid[207] with sekenes like as it was aforn, and I was as
baren and as drye as I never had comfort but litil. And as a
wretch I moned and hevyed for felyng of my bodily pey[n]es[208]
and for fayling of comfort, gostly and bodily. Than cam a
religious person to me and askid me how I ferid. And I seyd
I had ravid today, and he leuhe loud and inderly. And I seyd:
'The cross that stod afor my face, methowte it blode fast.' And
with this word the person that I spake to waxid al sad and
mervelid. And anon I was sor ashamid and astonyed for my
recleshede, and I thowte: 'This man takith sadly the lest word
that I myte seyen than saw I no mor therof.'[209] And whan I
saw that he toke it sadly and with so gret reverens, I wepid,[210]
ful gretly ashamid, and wold have ben shrevyn; but at that
tyme I cowde tell it no preist, for I thowte: 'How should a
preist levyn me?[211] I leve not our lord God.' This I levid
sothfastly for the tyme that I saw him, and so was than my
will and my menyng ever for done without end, but as a fole
I let it passyn from my mynd. A! lo I, wretch. This was a gret
synne, grete onkindness, that I for foly, of feling of a litill
bodily peyne, so onwisely lost for the time the comfort of all
this blissid shewing of our lord God. Here may you sene what
I am of myselfe; but herein wold our curtes lord not leve me.
And [I][212] lay still till night trosting in his mercy, and than I
gan to slepyn.[213] And in the slepe, at the begynnyng, methowte
the fend set him in my throte, puttand forth a visage ful nere
my face like a yong man; and it was longe and wonder lene;
I saw never none such. The color was rede like the tilestone
whan it is new brent, with blak spots therin like blak steknes,
fouler than the tilestone. His here was rode as rust, evisid
aforn, with syde lokks hongyng on the thounys. He grynnid
on me with a shrewd semelant, shewing white teeth; and so
mekil methowte it the more oggley. Body ne hands had he
none shaply, but with his pawes he held me in the throte and

would have stranglid me, but he myte not. This oggley shewing was made slepyng, and so was non other. And in all this time I trostid to be savid and kepid be the mercy of God. And our curtes lord gave me grace to waken, and onethis had I my lif. The persons that wer with me beheld me and wet my temples, and my herte began to comforten. And anon a lyte smoke came in the dore with a grete hete and a foule stinke. I said: 'Benedicite domine! It is al on fire that is here!' And I wened it had ben a bodily fire that shuld a brent us al to dede. I askid hem that wer with me if thei felt ony stynke. Thei seyd nay, thei felt none. I said 'Blissid be God!', for that wist I wele it was the fend that was comen to tempest me. And anon I toke to that our lord had shewid me on the same day, with al the feith of holy church, for I beheld it is bothen one, and fled therto as to my comforte. And anone al vanishid away, and I was browte to gret rest and peas withouten sekenes of body or drede of conscience.

67

Of the worshipfull syte of the soule, which is so nobly create that it myte no better a be made, in which the Trinite ioyeth everlastingly; and the soule may have rest in nothing but in God, which sittith therin reuling al things—lxvii chapter.[214]

And than our lord opened my gostly eye and shewid me my soule in midds of my herte. I saw the soule so large as it were an endles world and as it were a blisfull kyngdom; and be the conditions I saw therin I understode that it is a worshipful syte. In the midds of that syte sitts our lord Iesus, God and man, a faire person and of large stature, heyest bishopp, solemnest kinge, worshipfulliest lord; and I saw him clad solemnly and worshiply. He sitteth in the soule even ryte in peace and rest. And the Godhede ruleth and gemeth[215] hevyn and erth and all that is;[216] sovereyn myte, sovereyn wisedom, and sovereyn goodnes. The place that Iesus takith in our soule, he shal never removen it without end as to my syte; for in us

109

is his homliest home and his endles wonyng. And in this he shewid the lekyng that he hath of the makying of manys soule; for as wele as the Fader might make a creature, and as wele as the Son couth make a creature, so wele wold the Holy Gost that manys soule were made; and so it was don. And therfore the blissid Trinite enioyeth withouten end in the makyng of manys soule; for he saw fro without begynnyng what shuld liken him without end. Althing that he hath made shewith his lordship; as vnderstonding was geven at the same tyme be example of a creature that is to sen gret noblyes and king-domes longand to a lord, and whan it had sen al the noblyth beneathyn, then, merveling, it was sterid to seeke aboven to the hey place where the lord wonnyth, knowing be reason that his dwelling is in the worthyest place; and thus I vnderstode sothly that our soule may never have rest in things that is beneathin itselfe. And whan it cometh aboven all creatures into the selfe, yet may it not abyden in the beholdyng of the selfe, but all the beholding is blisfully sett in God that is the makar wonand therinn; for in manys soule is his very wonyng; and the heyest lyte and the brightest shynyng of the cite is the glorious love of our lord, as to my syte. And what may maken us more to enioyen in God tha[n][217] to sen in hym that he enioyeth heghest of al his werkes? For I saw in the same shewing that if the blisfull Trinite myte have made manys soule ony better, ony fairer, ony noblyer tha[n][218] it was made, he shuld not have be full plesid with the makyng of manys soule.[219] And he will that our herts ben mytyly reysid above the depeness of the erth and al vayne sorows, and enioyen in him.

68

Of sothfast knowing that it is Iesus that shewid all this and it was no ravyng, and how we owen to have sekir troste in all our tribulation that we shall not be overcome—lxviii chapter.

This was a delectable syte and a restfull shewyng: that it is so withouten end. And the beholding of this while we arn here, it is ful plesant to God and full gret spede to us. And the soule that thus beholdyth it makith it like to him that is beholdyn, and onyth it in rest and peas be his grace. And this was a singlar ioy and bliss to me that I saw him sitten; for the sekirnes of sitting shewith endles dwelling. And he gave me knowing sothfastly that it was he that shewid me al aforn. And whan I had beholden this with avisement, than shewid our good lord words full mekely withouten voice and withouten openyng of lipps, ryte as he had done, and said full swetely: 'Wete it now wele that it was no raveing that thou saw today, but take it and leve it, and kepe the therin and comfort the therwith and troste thou therto, and thou shalt not be overcome.' These last words wer seid for leryng of trew sekirness that it is our lord Iesus that shewid me all. And ryte as in the first worde that our good lord shewid, menyng his blissfull passion —'Herwith is the devill overcome'—ryte so he seid in the last word with full trew sekirness, menand us all: 'Thou shalt not ben overcommen.' And all this leryng in this trew comfort, it is generall to all my even cristen as it is afornseid, and so is Gods will. And these words: 'Thou shalt not ben overcome', was seid full sharply and full mightily for sekirness and comfort agens all tribulations that may comen. He seid not 'Thou shalt not be tempestid, thou shalt not be travelled, thou shalt not be disesid', but he seid: 'Thou shalt not be overcome.' God will that we taken heede at these words, and that we be ever myty in sekir troste, in wele and wo; for he lovith and lekyth us, and so will he that we love him and lekin him and mytily trosten in him; and al shal be wele. And sone after al was close and I sow no more.

69

Of the second long temptation of the devill to despeir, but she mytyly trosted to God and to the feith of holy church, rehersing the passion of Christe be the which she was deliverid—[lxix chapter.][220]

After this the fend came agen with his hete and with his stinke, and made me full besy; the stinke was so vile and so peynfull, and also dredfull and travellous. Also I heard a bodily iangeling as it had be of two bodies, and both, to my thynkyng, ianglyd at one time as if they had holden a parlement with a gret bysynes; and al was soft muttering, as I vnderstode nowte what they seid. And al this was to stirre me to dispeir, as methowte, semand to me as thei scornyd bidding of beds, which arn seid boistrosly with mouth, failing devowte entending and wise diligens the which we owen to God in our prayors. And our lord God gave me grace mytyly for to trosten in him, and to comforten my soule with bodily speech as I shuld have done to another person that had ben travelled. Methowte that bysynes myte not be likenyd to no bodily bysynes.[221] My bodily eye I sett in the same cross wher I had ben in comfort aforn that tyme, my tonge with speech of Crists passion and rehersing the feith of holy church, and myn hert to festen on God with al the trost and the myte. And I thowte to myselfe, menand: 'Thou hast now grete bysynes to kepe the in the feith, for thou shuldst not be taken of the enemy; woldst thou now for this time ever more be so bysy to kepe the fro synne, this were a good and a soverain occupation'; for I thowte sothly were I saf fro synne, I wer full saf fro all the fends of helle and enemys of my soule. And thus he occupyed me al that nyte, and on the morne till it was about prime day. And anon they wer all gone, all passid, and then left nothing but stinke; and that lested still awhile. And I scornyd him. And thus was I deliverd of hem be the vertue of Christ passion, for therwith is the fend overcome, as our lord Iesus Criste seid aforn.

70

In all tribulation we owe to be stedfast in the feith, trosting mytyly in God; for if our faith had no enimyte, it should deserve no mede; and how all these shewings arn in the faith—lxx chapter.

A Revelation of Love

In all this blissid shewing our good lord gave vnderstondyng
that the syte shuld passyn; which blissid shewing the feith
kepith, with his owne good will and his grace; for he left with
me neyther signe nor token wherby I myte knowen it, but he
left with me his owne blissid worde in true vnderstondyng,
byddand me full mytyly that I shuld leven it. And so I do;
blissied mot he ben! I beleve that he is our savior that shewid
it, and that it is the feith that he shewid. And therfore I leve
it enioyand; and therto I am bounden be al his own menyng,
with the next words that folowen: 'Kepe the therein and
comfort the therewith and trost thou therto.' Thus I am
bounden to kepen it in my feith. For on the selfe day that it
was shewid, what time that the syte was passid, as a wretch I
forsoke it and openly I seid that I had ravid. Than our lord
Iesus of his mercy wold not letten it perish, but he shewid it
al agen within, in my soule, with mor fulhede, with the blissid
lyte of his pretious love, seyand these word full mytyly and
full mekely: 'Witt it now wele, it was no raving that thou saw
this day', as if he had seid: 'For the syte was passid fro, the
lestist it and couthest not kepe it; but witt it now, that is to
sey, now that thou seest it.' This was seid not only for the
same time, but also to setten therupo[n]²²² the ground of my
feith where he seith anon folowing: 'But take it, leve it, and
kepe the therin and comfort the therwith and trost thou therto;
and thou shalt not be overcome.'²²³ In these vi words that
folowen, 'Take it', his menyng is to festyn it feyfully in our
herte; for he will that it dwell with us in feith to our lifes end,
and after in fulhede of ioy, willand that we have ever sekir
trost in his blisfull behests, knowyng his goodness; for our feith
is conntried in divers manners be our owne blin[d]hede²²⁴ and
our gostly enemy, within and without, and therfore our
pretious lover helpith us with gostly syte and trew teching on
sundry manners, within and without, wereby that we may
know him. And therfore in what manner he techith us, he will
we peceivyn him wisely, receivyn him swetely and kepin us in
hym feithfully; for aboven the feith is no goodnes kept in this
life, as to my sight; and beneath the feith is no helpe of soule;
but in the feith: there will the lord that we kepe us. For we

113

have be his goodnes and his owne werkeing to kepe us in the feith and, be his suffrance, be gostly enmyte we are assayed in the feith and made myty; for of our feith had none enmyte it should deserve no mede, as to the vnderstondyng that I have in all our lords menyng.

71

Glad and mery and sweete is the blisfull lovely cher of our lord to our souleis; for he havith us ever lifand in lovelongeing, and he will our soule be in glad cher to him to gevin him his mede. And thus I hope with his grace he hath, and more shall, draw in, the vtter chere to the inner cher, and maken us all at one with him and ech of us with other, in trew lestand ioye that is Ihesus. I have menyng of iii manner of cheres of our lord. The first is cher of passion as he shewid while he was here in this lif, deyand. Thow this beholdyng be mornyng and swemful, yet it is glad and mery, for he is God. The ii manner of chere is pite and ruth and compassion; and this shewith he to all his lovers with sekirnes of keping that have[226] to his mercy. The iii is the blisfull cher as it shal be without end; and this was oftenest and lengest continuid. And thus in the time of our peyne and our wo he shewith us chere of his passion and of his cross, helpand us to berer[227] by his owne blissid vertue. And in the time of our synnyng he shewith to us chere of ruth and pite, mytily kepand us and defending [agaynst][228] all our enemies. And these ii be the common cher which he shewith to us in this life; therewith medlarid the thord, and that is his blisfull chere, like in parte as it shall be in hevyn. And that is a gracious touchyng and swete lyteyng of the gostly lefe wherby that we arn kept in sekir feith, hope and charite, with contrition and devotion and also with contemplation and

114

[alle manner]²²⁹ of true solace and swete comforts. The blisfull chere of our lord God werkith it in us be grace.

72

*Synne in the chosen soulis is dedly for a tyme, but thei be not ded in the syght of God; and how we have here matter of ioy and moneing, and that for our blindhede and weyte of flesh; and of the most comfortable chere of God; and why these shewings were made—lxxii chapter.*²³⁰

But now behovith me to tellen in what manner I saw synne dedly in the creatures which shall not dyen for synne, but liven in the ioy of God without end. I saw that ii contrareties should never be to God²³¹ in one stede. The most contrious that arn, is the heyest bliss and the depest peyne. The heyest bliss that is, is to have him in cleerty of endless life, him verily seand, him swetely feland, all perfectly haveand in fulhede of ioy. And thus was the blisfull cheere of our lord shewid in pite; in which shewing I saw that synne is most contrarie, so ferforth that as long as we be medled with ony part of synne we shall never see cleerly the blisfull cheere of our lord. And the horibler and the greivouser that our synnes bene, the deeper are we for that time fro this blisfull syte. And therfore it semith to us oftentimes as we wern in peril of deth, in a party of hell, for the sorow and peyne that the synne is to us. And thus we arn ded for the tyme fro the very syte of our blisfull life, But in all this I saw sothfastly that we be not dede in the syte of God, ne he passith never fro us; but he shall never have his full bliss in us till we have our full bliss in him, verely seand his faire blisfull chere; for we arn ordeynid therto in kinde, and gettyn therto be grace. Thus I saw how synne is dedly for a short time in the blissid creatures of endless life. And ever the more clerely that the soule seith this blisfull chere be grace of loveyng, the more it longyth to seen it in fullhede;²³² for notwithstonding that our lord God wonnyth in us and is here with us, and al he halsith us and beclosith us for tender love

115

that he may never levyn us, and is more nere to us than tongue can tellen or herte can thynken, yet may we never stint of moning nor of weping ne of longyng til whan we see him cleerly in his blissfull chere; for in that pretious, blisfull syte there may no wo abiden ne no wele failen. And in this I saw matter of myrth and matter of monyng: matter of myrthe, for our lord our maker is so nere to us and in us, and we in him, be sekirne[s]²³³ of keping of his grete goodnes; matter of monyng, for our gostly eye is so blinde and we be so born downe be weyte of our dedly flesh and derkhede of synne that we may not sen our lord God clerly in his faire blisful chere. No, and because of this myrkehede unethes we can leven and trowen his grete love, our sekirness of keping; and therefore it is that I sey we may never stinten of moning ne of wepyng. This weping meneth not al in poryng out of teares by our bodily eye, but also to more gostly vnderstonyng; for the kindly desire of our soule is so gret and so onmesurable that if it were goven us to our solace and to our comfort al the noblyth that ever God made in hevyn and in erth, and we saw not the fair blisfull chere of hymselfe, yet we shuld not stynten of moning ne of gostly weping, that is to sey, of peynfull longing, till whan we sen verily the faire blisfull chere of our maker. And if we were in all the peyne that herte can thy[n]ke²³⁴ and tongue may tell, if we myten in that time sen his faire, blisfull chere, all this peyn shuld us not agrevin. Thus is that blisfull syte end of all manner of peyne to lovand soule, and fulfilling all manner of ioy and bliss. And that shewid he in the hey, mervelous words wher he seyd: 'I it am that is heyest; I it am that is lowist; I it am that is all.' It longith to us to have iii manner of knowyngs: the first is that we knowen our lord God; the ii that we knowen ourselfe, what we arn be him in kinde and grace; the iii that we knowen mekely what ourselfe is anempts our synne and febilness. And for these iii was all the shewing made, as to my vnderstondyng.

73

These revelations were shewid iii wises; and of ii gostly [sekenes][235] of which God will we amend us, remembring his passion, knowing also he is al love; for he will we have sekirnes and liking in love, not takyng onskilfull hevyness for our synnes past—lxxiii chapter.[236]

All the blissid teching of our lord God was shewid be iii partes: that is to sey, by bodily syte, and by word formyd in myn vnderstondyng, and be gostly sight. For the bodily seyte, I have seid as I saw as trewly as I can; and for the words, I have seid them rith as our lord shewid hem to me; and for the gostly syght, I have seyd sumdele, but I may neve[r][237] full tellen it, and therefore of this syght I am sterrid to sey more as God will give me grace. God shewid ii manner of sekenes that we have: that on is onpatience or slaith, for we bere our trevell and our pey[n]es[238] hevily; that other is dispeir or doubtfull drede, as I shall seyen after. Generally he shewid synne wherin that all is comprehendid, but in special he shewid not but thes two. And these ii arn thei that most travelin and tempesten us, as be that our lord shewid me, of which he will we be amendid; I speake of swich men and women that for God love haten synne and disposen hem to do Gods will; than be our gostly blindhede and bodily hevynes, we arn most enclinand to these; and therfore it is Gods will thei be knowen and than shall we refusen hem as we don other synnes. And full helpe of this ful mekely our lord shewid, the patience that he had in his herd passion, and also the ioyeing and the likyng that he hath of that passion for love. And this shewid in example that we shuld gladly and wisely baren our pey[n]es;[239] for that is gret plesing to him and endless profitt to us. And the cause why we arn trevellid with them is for onknoweing of love. Thow the iii persons in the Trinite ben all even in the selfe, and the soule toke most vnderstonding in love; ya, and he will in allthing that we have our beholding and our enioyeyng in

117

love. And of this knoweyng arn we most blynde; for som of us leven that God is almyty and may don all, and that he is al wisdam and can don all, but that he is all love and will don all, there we astynten. And this unknowing, it is that that lettith most Gods lovers, as to my syte; for whan we begynnen to haten synne and amenden us be the ordinance of holy church, yet ther dwellith a drede that lettith us, for the beholding of ourselfe and of our synnes aforn don, and sum of us for our everydayly synnes; for we hold nor our covenants ne kepe not our cleness that our lord settith us in, but fallen oftentimes in so much wretcidness that shame it is to seen it. And the beholding of this makyth us sorry and so hevy that onethis we can finde ony comfort. And this drede we taken sumtime for a mekness, but this is a foule blyndhed and a waykenes. And we cannot dispisen it as we don another[r][240] synne that we knowen,[241] for it commyth of enmite. And it is agen truth; for of all the propertes of the blisfull Trinite it is God will that we have most sekirnes and likeing in love; for love makith myte and wisdam full meke to us; for ryte as be the curtesye of God he forgivith our synne afte[r][242] the tyme that we repenten us, ryte so will he that we forgiven our synne as anempts our unskilfull hevyness and our doutfull dreds.

74

There ben iiii manner of drede, but reverent drede is a lovely true that never is without meke love; and yet thei be not both one; and how we should pray God for the same—lxxiiii chapter.

For I vnderstond iiii manner dreds. One is the drede of afray that cummith to a man sodenly be frelte. This drede doith good, for it helpith to purge man as doeth bodily sekenes or swich other peyne that is not synne; for all swich peynys helpe man if thei be patiently taken. The ii is drede of peyne wherby man is sterid and wakid fro sleepe of synne;[243] he is not abil for the time to perceivyn the soft comfort of the Holy Gost till he have vnderstonding of this drede of peyne, of bodily

deth and of gostly enemyes. And this drede stirrith us to seken
comfort and mercy of God; and thus this drede helpith us to
sekyn comfort and mercy of God and abileth us to have
contrition be the blisfull touching of the Holy Gost. The iii is
doubtfull drede. Doutfull drede, in as mech as it drawith to
dispeir, God will have it turnyd in us into love be the knowing
of love; that is to sey, that the bitternes of doubt be turnyd
into sweteness of kinde love be grace; for it may never plesyn
our lord that his servants douten in his goodnes. The iiii is
reverent drede, for there is no drede that fully plesith God in
us but reverent drede; and that is full soft, for the more it is
had, the less is it felt for swetenes of love. Love and drede
are brethren; and thei arn rotid in us be the goodnes of our
maker and thei shall never be taken fro us without end. We
have of kinde to loven and we have of grace to loven; and we
have of kinde to dreden and we have of grace to dreden. It
longith to the lordshippe and to the faderhede to be dred, as
it longith to the goodness to be lovid; and it longith to us that
arn his servants and his children to dreden him for lordshipp
and faderhede, as it longith to us to loven him for goodhede.
And thow this reverent drede and love be not partid asundre,
yet thei arn not both one, but thei arn ii in properte and in
werking and neither of them may be had without other.
Therfore I am sekir he that lovith, he dredith, thow that he
fele it but a littil. All dreds other than reverent drede that arn
proferid to us, thow they come under the collor of holyness,
yet arn not so trew; and hereby may they be knowen
asu[n]der.[244] That drede that makith us hastily to fleen from
all that is not good and fallen into our lords brest as the child
into the moder barme, with all our entent and with all our
mynd knowand our febilness and our gret nede, knowing his
everlesting goodnes and his blisfull love, only sekeing to him
for salvation, clevand to with sekir troste—that drede that
bringith us into this werking, it is kinde, gracious, good and
true. And all that contraries to this, either it is wronge, or it
is medlid with wronge. Than is this the remedye, to knowen
hem both and refusen the wrong. For the kinde profitt of drede
which we have in this lif be the gracious werking of the Holy

119

Gost, the same shall be in hevyn aforn God, gentill, curtes and ful delectabil. And thus we shall in love be homley and nere to God, and we shall in drede be gentil and curtes to God; and both alike evyn. Desir we of our lord God to dredin him reverently and to love him mekely and to trosten in him mytyly; for whan we drede him reverently and loven him mekely our troste is never in vaine; for the more that we trosten and the mytylier, the more we plesyn and worshippe our lord that we trosten in. And if us feile this reverent drede and meke love (as God forbode we should) our trost shall sone be misrulid for the tyme. And therefore us nedith mekil for to prayen our lord of grace that we may have this reverent drede and meke love, of his gift, in herte and in werke; for withouten this no man may plesyn God.

75

Us nedith love, longing and pite, and of iii manner of longing in God which arn in us; and how in the day of dome the ioy of the blissid shal ben incresid, seing verily the cause of allthyng that God hath don, dredfully tremeland and thankand for ioye, mervelyng the gretnes of God [and][245] *lulshed*[246] *of all that is made—lxxv chapter.*

I saw that God may done all that us nedith; and these iii that I shall seyen, neden: love, longing, pite. Pite in love kepith us in time of our nede, and longing in the same love drawith us into hevyn; for the threist of God is to have the general man into him, in which thrist he hath [drawyn][247] his holy that be now in bliss; and gettand his lively members, ever he drawith and drinkith, and yet he thristith and longith. I saw iii manner of longing in God, and al to one end; of which we have the same in us, and of the same vertue, and for the same end. The ist is for that he longyth to learn us to knowen him and loven him evermore, as it is convenient and spedefull to us. The ii is that he longith to have us up to his bliss as soules arn whan thei arn taken out of peyne into hevyn. The iii is to fulfillen

120

us in bliss; and that shall be on the last day fulfillid ever to lesten; for I saw, as it is knowne in our feith, that the peyne and sorow shall be endid to all that shall be savid. And not only we shall recevyn the same bliss the soule aforne have had in hevyn, but also we shall receive anew, which plenteously shal be flowing out of God into us and fulfillen us; and this be the goods which he hath ordeynid to geve us from without begynnyng; these goods are tresurid and hidde in hymselfe; for into that time, creature is not myty ne worthy to receivin them. In this we shall seen verily the cause of allthyng he hat don; and evermore we shall seen the cause of all things that he hath suffrid. And the bliss and the fulfilling shall be so deepe and so hey that for wonder and mervell all creatures shal have to God so gret reverent drede, overpassing that hath been seen and felt beforn, that the pillers of hevyn shall tremelyn and quakyn. But this manner of tremelyng and drede shall have no peyne; but it longith to the worthy myte of God thus to be beholden of his creatures, dredfully tremeland and quakand for mekehede of ioye, mervelyng at the greatnes of God the maker, and of the litilhede of all that is made; for the beholdyng of this makith the creature mervelous meke and mylde. Wherfore God will, and also it longith to us, both in kynde and grace, to witten and knowen of this, desirand this syte and this werking; for it ledith us in ryte wey and kepith us in true life and onyth us to God. And as good as God is, as gret he is; and as mekil as it longith to his Godhede to be lovid, so mekill it longyth to his grethede to be dredid; for this reverent drede is the faire curtesie that is [in][248] hevyn aforn Gods face. And as mekil as he shall than be knowen and lovid overpassing that he is now, in so mekill he shall be dredid overpassing that he is now. Wherfore it behovith needs to ben that all hevyn and erth shall tremelyn and quaken when the pillars shall tremelyn and quaken.

76

I speke but littil of reverent drede, for I hope it may be seen in this matter afornseid. But wele I wot our lord shewid me no soules but those that dred him; for wele I wott the soule that trewly taketh the techyng of the Holy Gost, it hatith more synne for vilehede and horibilite than it doth all the peyne that is in hell; for the soule that beholdith the kindenes of our lord Iesus, it hatith non helle but synne, as to my sygte. And therefore it is Goddis will that we knowen synne, and prayen bysyly and travellyn willfully and sekyn, teching mekely, that we fall not blindly therin; and if we fallen, that we risen redily, for it is the most peyne that the soule may have, to turne fro God ony time be synne. The soule that will be in rest, whan other mannys synne commith [to mynde],[249] he shall fleen it as the peyne of helle, seking into God for remedy, for helpe [agayne][250] it; for the beholdyng of other mannys synnes, it makith as it were a thick myst aforne the eye of the soule, and we may not for the tyme se the fairehede of God, but if we may beholden hem with contrition with him, with compassion on him and with holy desire to God for hem; for withouten this it noyith and tempestith and lettith the soule that beholdith hem; for this [I][251] vnderstode in the shewing of compassion. In this blisfull shewing of our lord I have vnderstondyng of ii contaries: that one is the most wisdam that ony creture may done in this life; that other is the most foly. The wisdam is creature to done after the wille and councell of his heyest sovereyn freind. This blissid freind is Ihesus; and it is his will and his councell that we holden us with him and settyn us to him, homley, evermore, in what state so we ben;

122

for whether so that we ben foule or clene, we arn al one in his loveing. For wele ne for wo he will never we fleen him; but for the chongeabilitie that we arn in in ourselfe we fallen often into synne. Than we have this be the stering of our enemy, be our owne foly and blyndhede; for they seien thus: 'Thou wittest wele thou art a wretch, a synner, and also ontrew; for thou kepist not the command; thou behotist oftentymes our lord that thou shalt don better, and anon after, thou fallist agen in the same, namely in slauth, in lesyng of tyme'; for that is the begynning of synne, as to my syghte, and namely to the creatures that have goven hem to serven our lord with inward beholding of his blissid goodness. And this makith us adred to apear afore our curtes lord. Than is it our enemy that will putt us on bakke with his false drede of our writchidnes, for peyne that he threatith us by; for it is his menyng to make us so hevy and so wery in this that we shuld lettyn out of mende the fair, blisfull beholdyng of our everlasting freind.

77

Off the enmite of the fend, which lesith more in our uprising than he winnith be our fallyng, and therfore he is scornyd; and how the scorge of God shuld be suffrid with mynde of his passion, for that is spe[c]ially[252] rewardid aboven penance be ourself chosen; and we must nedes hove wo, but curtes God is our leder, keper and bliss—lxxvii chapter.

Our good lord shewid the enmite of the fend, wherby I understode that all that is contrarious to love and to pece, it is the fend and of his parte. And we have of our febilnes and our foly to fallen, and we have of mercy and grace of the Holy Gost to risen to more ioye. And if our eneme owte wynnith of us be our fallyng, for it is his likenes, he lesith manyfold more in our rising be charite and mekenes. And this glorious riseing, it is to him so gret sorow and peyne, for the hate that [he][253] hath to our soule, that he brynnyt continuly in envy.

123

And al this sorow that he wold maken us to have, it shal turne
to himselfe. And for this it was that our lord scornyd him; and
this made me mytyly to lauhen. Than is this the remedy: that
we ben aknowen [of][254] our writchidnes and flen to our lord;
for ever the more redier that we ben, the more spedefull it is
to us to neyghen him. And sey we thus in our mening: 'I know
wele I have a shrewid peyne, but our lord is almyty and may
punish me mytyly, and he is al wisdam and can punish me
skilfully, and he is all goodnes and lovith me full tendirly.'
And in this beholdyng it is necessarye for us to abeyden; for
it is a lovely mekeness of a synful soule, wroute be mercy and
grace of the Holy Gost, whan we will willfully and gladly taken
the scorge and chastening of our lord himselfe will geve us.
And it shal be full tendir and full esy if that we will onely
holden us paid with him and with all his werkes; for the
pennance that mon taketh of himselfe was not shewid me: that
is to sey, it was not shewid specifyed; but it was shewid specialy
and heyly and with full lovely chere that we shall mekely and
patiently beryn and suffren the penance that God himselfe
gevith us, with mynde in his blissid passion; for whan we have
mend in his blissid passion, with pite and love, than we suffren
with him like as his freinds did that seen it, and [this][255] was
shewid in the xiii, ner at the begynnyng, wher it spekith of
pite; for he seith: 'Accuse not [thy]selfe[256] overdon mekil,
demandand that tribulation and thy wo is al for thy defaute;
for I will not that thou be hevye ne sorowfull vndiscretly; for
I tell the how so tho do, thou shalt have wo. And therfore I
will that thou wisely know thi penance, and shalt then sothly
seene that all thi living is penance profitable. This place is
prison and this lif is penance, and in the remedy he will we
enioyen. The remedy is that our lord is with us, kepand and
ledand into the fulhede of ioye; for this is an endless ioy to
us in our lords menyng, that he that shall ben our bliss whan
we arn there, he is our keper while we arn here. Our wey and
our hevyn is trew love and sekir troste; and of this he gaf
understonding in all, and namly in the shewing of his passion
wher he made me mytyly to chesin him for my hevyn. Fle we
to our lord and we shall be comfortid; touch we him and we

124

shall be made clene; cleve to him and we shall be sekir and safe fro al maner of peril; for our curtes lord will that we ben as homley with him as herte may thinke or soule may desiren. But beware that we taken not so reklesly this homleyhede that we levyn curtesy; for our lord himselfe is sovereyn homley-hede, and as homley as he is, as curtes he is; for he is very curtes. And the blissid creatures that shall ben in hevyn with him without end, he will have hem like to himselfe in all things. And to be like our lord perfectly, it is our very salvation and our full bliss. And if we wott not how we shall don all this, desire we of our lord and he shal lerne us; for it [is]²⁵⁷ his owne likeing and his worship. Blissid mot he be!

78

Our lord will we know iiii manner of goodnes that he doith to us, and how we neede the lyte of grace to knowen our synne and febilnes, for we arn nothing of ourselfe but writchidnes, and we may now know the horribilnes of synne as it is; and how our enemy would we should never know our synne till the last day, wherfore we arn mekil bowndend to God that shewith it now—lxxviii chapter.

Our lord of his mercy shewith us our synne and our febilnes be the swet gracious lyte of hymselfe; for our synne is so vile and so horrible that he²⁵⁸ of his curtesie will not shew it to us but be the lyte of his grace and mercy. Of iiii things it is his will that we have knowing: the first is that he is our ground of whom we have all our life and our being; the ii, that he kepeth us mytyly and mercifully in the tyme that we arn in our synne and monge all our enemies that arn full fel upon us—and so mekil we arn in the more peril for we geven him occasion therto and kno not our owne nede; the iii is how curtesly he kepith us and makith us to knowen that we gon amyss; the iiii is how stedfastly he abidith us and chongith no chere, for he will that we be turnyd and onyd to him in love as he is to us. And thus be this gracious knoweing we may

125

seen our synne profitably without despeir; for sothly us nedith
to seen it; and be the syte we shall be made ashamd of ourselfe
and broken downe as anempts our pride and presumtion; for
us behovith verily to seen that of ourselfe we arn ryte nowte
but synne and wretchiddnes. And thus be the syte of the less
that our lord shewith us, the more is wastid which we se not;
for he of his curtesye mesurith the syte to us, for it is so vile
and so horrible that we shuld not enduren to seen it as it is.
And be this meke knowing thus, throw contrition and grace
we shall be broken fro all things that is not our lord, and than
shall our blissid saviour perfectly helyn us and one us to him.
This breking and this helyng our lord menith be the general
man; for he that is heyest and nerest with God, he may seen
himselfe synnefull, and nedith, with me; and I that am the lest
and lowest of those that shall be save, I may be comfortid with
him that is heyest. So hath our lord onyd us in charite whan
he shewid me that I shuld synne. And for ioy that I had in
beholdyng of him I entend not redily to that shewing; and our
curtis lord stynte than and wold not ferther tech me till that
he gave me grace and will to entenden. And hereof was I lerid,
thow that we be heyly lifted up into contemplation be the
special geft of our lord, yet us behovith nedis therwith to
have knoweing and syte of our synne and our febilnes; for
withouten this knowing we may not have trew mekenes, and
without this we may not be savid. And also I saw that we may
now have this knowing of ourself, ne of none of all our gostly
enemies, for thei will us not so mekil good; for if it wer be
their will, we should not seen it into our endyng day. Than be
we mekil bounden to God that he will himselfe for love shewen
it us in time of mercy and grace.

79

*We are lernyd to our synne, and not to our neighbors, but for
their helpe; and God will we know whatsomever stering we have
contrary to this shewing, it comith of our enemy; for the gret
l[o]ve*[259] *of God knowen, we should not ben the more reckles*

to fallen, and if we fallen we must hastely risen or ell we are gretly onkind to God—lxxix chapter.

Also I had in this more vnderstondyng: in that he shewid me that I should synne, I toke it nakidly to myne owne singular person, for I was none otherwise stirrid at that time; but be the hey, gracious comfort of our lord that followid after, I saw that his menyng was for the general man, that is to sey, all man which is synfull and shall ben into the last day; of which man I am a member, as I hope, be the mercy of God; for the blissid comfort that I saw, it is large enow for us all. And here was I lerid that I shuld se myn owne synne and not other mens synns but if it may be for comfort and helpe of myn evin Cristen. And also in this same shewing, where I saw that I shuld synne, there was I leryd to be dredfull for onsekirness of myselfe; for I wott not how I shall fallen, nor I know not the mesurre ner the gretness of synne; for that wold I have wist dredfully, and therto I had non answere. Also our curtes lord, in the same tyme, he shewid full sekirly and mytyly the endleshede and the onchongeabilitie of his love; and alsa, be his gret goodnes and his grace inwardly keping, that the love of him and our soule shal never be departid in two, without end. And thus in this drede I have matter of mekeness that savith me from presumption; and in the blissid shewing of love I have matter of tru comfort and of ioy that savith me fro dispeir. All this homley shewing of our curtes lord, it is a lovely lesson and a swete, gracious teching of himselfe in comforting of our soule; for he will that we knowen, be the swetenes and homley loveing of him, that all that we seen or felyn, within or without, which is contrarious to this is of the enemy and not of God; as thus: if we be stered to be the more recles of our living or of the keping of our herts be the same cause that we have knowing of this plenteous love, than needs us gretly to beware; for this stering, if it come, it is ontrew, and gretly we owen to haten it, for it all hath no likeness of Gods will. And whan that we be fallen be frelte or blyndhede, than our curtes lord touchith us, stireth us and clepith us; and than will he that we seen our wretchidness and mekely ben it aknowen.

127

But he will not we abiden thus, ne he will not that we beseyn us gretly about our accusing, nor he will not that we ben wretchfull of ourselfe; but he will that we hastily entenden to him; for he stondyth al alufe and abideth us swemefully and moningly till whan we come, and hath hast to have us to him; for we arn his ioy and his deligte, and he is our salve and our life. Tho I sey he stondyth al alone, I leve the speking of the blissid company of hevyn and speke of his office and his werking here on erth, upon the condition of the [shewyng].[260]

80

By iii thyngs God is worshippid and we savid; and how our knowing now is but as an ABC; and swete Ihesus doith all, abyding and monyng with us, but whan we arn in synne Christ monyth alone, than it longith to us, for kindness and reverens, hastely to turne agen to him—lxxx chapter.

Be iii things man stondith in this life; be which iii God is worshipped and we be spedid, kept and savid. The ist is use of manys reason naturall; the ii is commen teching of holy church; the thred is inward gracious werking of the Holy Gost; and these iii ben all of one God. God is the ground of our kindly reason; and God, the teaching of holy church; and God is the Holy Gost. And all ben sundry gifts to which he will we have gret regard and attenden us therto; for these werkyn in us continualy all to God,[261] and these ben grete thyngs; of which gret things he will we have knowing here as it were in one ABC: that is to seyn, that we have a litill knoweing, whereof we shall have fullhede in hevyn; and that is for to spede us. We knowen in our feith that God alone toke our kinde and non but he; and ferthermore, that Criste allone did all the werks that longin to our salvation, and none but he; and ryte so he alone doith now the last end: that is to sey, he wonny[t]h[262] here with us and rulith us and governith us in this lifing, and bringith us to his bliss. And thus shall he doe as long as ony soule is in erth that shall come to hevyn; and so ferforth that if ther wer no suich soule but one, he shuld be with all alone till he had brought up to his bliss. I leve and vnderstond the ministration of angells as clerks tellen, but it was not shewid me; for himselfe is nerest and mekest, heyest and lowest, and doith all; and not only all that us neds, but also he doith all that is worshipfull, to our ioy in hevyn. And wher I sey he abidith swemefully and monyng, it menyth all the trew felyng that we have in ourselfe in contrition and compassion, and all sweming and monyng that we are not onyd with our lord. And all swich that is spedfull, it is Christ in us; and thow some of us fele it seldam, it passith never fro Criste till what tyme he hath browte us out of all our wo; for love suffrith never to be without pite. And what tyme that we fallen into synne and leve the mynd of him and the keping of our own soule, than kepith Criste alone al the charge of us; and thus stondith he swemely and monyng. Than longith it to us for reverence and kindeness to turne us hastely to our lord and levyen him not alone. He is here alone with us all: that is to sey, only for us he is here. And what tyme I am strange to him be synne, dispeir or slawth, than I let my lord stonden alone, in as mekill as it is in me; and thus it farith with us all which ben synners. But thow it be so that we do thus oftentimes, his goodnes suffrith us never to be alone; but lestingly he is with us, and tenderly he excusith us, and ever sheildith us fro blame in his syte.

81

This blissid woman saw God in divers manners, but she saw him take no resting place but in manys soule; and he will we enioyen more in his love then sorowen for often falling, remembring reward everlasting, and liveing gladly in penance; and why God suffrith synne—lxxxi chapter.

Our good lord shewid him in dyvers manners, both in hevyn, in erth, but I saw him take no place but in mannys soule. He shewid him in erth in the swete incarnation and in his blissid passion. And in other manner he shewid him in erth wher I sey: 'I saw God in a poynte.' And in other manner he shewid him in erth thus as it were in pilegrimage: that is to sey, he is here with us, ledand us, and shal ben till whan he hath browte us all to his bliss in hevyn. He shewid him dyvers tymes reynand, as it is afornseyd, but principally in mannys soule. He hath taken there his resting place and his worshipfull cyte; out of which worshipfull see he shall never risen nor removen without end. Mervelous and solemne is the place wher the lord wonnyth. And therefore he will that we redily entenden to his gracious touching, more enioying in his hole love than sorrowand in our often fallings; for it [is][263] the most worshippe to him of onything that we may don, that we leven gladly and meryly, for his love, in our penance; for he beholdith us so tendirly that he seith all our liveing and penance; for kind loveand is to him ay lestand penance in us, which penance he werkith in us and mercifully he helpith us to baren it; for his love makith him to longyn, his wisdam and his trewth with his rytfulhede makith him to suffren us here, and in this manner he will seene it in us; for this is our kindly penance and the heyest, as to my syte, for this penance commith never fro us till what tyme that we be fullfilled whan we shal have him to our mede. And therefore he will that we setten our herts in the overpassing: that is to sey, fro the peyne that we felen into the bliss that we trosten.

82

God beholdith the monyng of the soule with pite and not with blom,[264] and yet we do nowte but synne, in which we arn kept in solace and in drede; for he will we turne us to him, redy clevand to his love, seand that he is our medicyne; and so we must love, in longing and in enioyeing; and whatsoever is contrarie to this is not of God but of enmity—lxxxii chapter.

But here shewid our curtis lord the moneing and the morning of the soule, menand thus: 'I wote wele thou wilt liven for my

love merily and gladly suffrand all the penance that may com
to the, but in as mech as thou livest not without synne,[265] thou
woldest suffre for my love all the wo, all the tribulation and
disese that myte come to the. And it is soth. But be not mekill
agreved with synne that fallith to the agens thy will.' And here
I vnderstode that: that the lord beholdith the servant with pite
and not with blame, for this passing lif askith not to liven al
withoute blame and synne. He loveith us endlesly, and we
synne customably, and he shewith us full myldely; and than
we sorow and mornen discretly, turnand us into the beholding
of his mercy, clevand to his love and goodness, seand that he
is our medecine, wittand that we doe nowte but synne. And
thus be the mekeness that we getten be the syte of our synne,
feythfully knowing his everlasting love, him thanking and
prayseing, we plesyn him. 'I love the and thou lovist me; and
our love shall not be departid in two, and for thi profitt I
suffre.' And all this was shewid in gostly vnderstondyng
sayand these blissid words: 'I kepe the full sekerly.' And be
gret desire that I have in our blissid lord that we shal leven
in this manner, that is to sey, in longing and enioyeng, as all
this lesson of love shewith, therby I vnderstode that all that
is contrarious to us is not of him, but of enmyte; and he will
that we knowen it be the swete gracious lyt of his kynde love.
If any swich lover be in erth which is continuly kept fro falling,
I know it not, for it was not shewid me. But this was shewid:
that in falling and in ryseing we arn eve[r][266] preciously kept
in one love; for in the beholding of God we fall not, in the
beholding of selfe we stond not, and both these ben soth, as
to my syte; but beholdyng of our lord God is the heyest
sothnes; than arn we mekil bound to God that he will in this
living shewin us this hey sothness. And I understode that while
we be in this life, it is full spedefull to us that we sen both
these at onys; for the heyer beholding kepith us in gostly solace
and trew enioying in God; that other, that is the lower
beholding, kepith us in drede and makith us ashamyd of
ourselfe. But our good lord will ever that we beholden us
mekil more in beholdyng of the heyer, and not levyn the
knowing of the lower, into the time that we [be][267] browte up

above, wher we shall have our lord Ihesus onto our mede, and ben fulfillid of ioy and bliss withoute end.

83

Of iii properties in God, life, love and light; and that our reason is in God accordand; it is heyest gift; and how our feith is a light commeing of the Fader, mesurid to us, and in this night us ledand; and the end of our wo; sodenly our eye shall be openid in full light and clerte of syte, which is our maker, fader and Holy Gost in Ihesus our saviour—lxxxiii chapter.

I had in parte touching, sight and feling in iii propertes of God, in which the strength and effect of all the revelation stondith; and thei were seene in every shewing, and most propirly in the xii, wher it seith oftentimes ['I it am.']²⁶⁸ The properties are these: lif, love and ligte. In life is mervelous homlihede, and in love is gentil curtesye, and in lyte is endless kyndhede. These propertes were in on goodness; into which goodnes my reason wold ben onyd and cleve to with all the myte. I beheld with reverent drede, and heyly mervelyng in the syte and in the feling of the swete accord that our reason is in God, vnderstondyng that it is the heyest gifte that we have receivid, and it is groundid in kinde. Our feith is a light, kindly command of our endles day, that is our fader, God; in which light our moder, Criste, and our good lord the Holy Gost ledith us in this passand life. This light is mesurid discretly, nedefully standand to us in the night. The light is cause of our life, the night is cause of our peyne and of al our wo, in which we deserven mede and thanks of God; for we, with mercy and grace, wilfuly knowen and leven our light, goeand therin wisely and mytyly. And at the end of wo, sodenly our eye shall ben openyd, and in clerte of light our sight shall be full; which light is God our maker and Holy Gost in Christ Ihesus our savior. Thus I saw and vnderstode that our feith is our light in our night; which light is God our endless day.

84

Charite is this light, which is not so litil but that it is [m]ede-
full,[269] *with travel, to deserven endles worshipfull thanke of*
God; for feith and hope leden us to charite, which is in iii
manners—lxxxiiii chapter.

The light is charite, and the mesuring of this light is don to us
profitably by the wisdam of God; for neyther the light is so
large that we may seen our blisfull day, ne it is sperid fro us,
but it is suich a light in which we may liven medefully, w[i]th[270]
travel deservand the endless worship of God. And this was
seen in the vi shewing where he seid: 'I thank the [of]271 thi
service and of thi travell.' Thus charite kepith us in feith and
in hope; and hope ledith us in charite. And at the end al shall
be charite. I had iii manner of vnderstonding in this light,
charite: the first is charite onmade; the second is charite made;
the iii is charite goven. Charite onmade is God; charite made
is our soule in God; charite goven is vertue; and that is a
gracious geft of werking in which we loven God for himselfe
and ourselves in God and that God loveth, for God.

85

God lovid his chosen fro without begynning, and he never[r][272]
suffrith them to be hurte wherof their bliss might be lessid; and
how privities now hidde in hevyn shall be knowen, wherefore
we shall bliss our lord that everything is so wele ordeynid
—lxxxv chapter.

And in this sight I merveled heyley; for notwithstondyng our
simple liveing and our blindhede here, yet endlesly our curtes
lord beholdith us in this workeing, enioyand. And of allthing
we may plesin him best wisely and truely to levin it and to
enioyen with him and in him; for as verily as we shall ben in

the bliss of God withouten end, him praysand and thankand, as verily we have ben in the foresight of God lovid and knowen in his endless purpose fro withouten begynning; in which onbegunne love he made us, and in the same love he kepith us and never suffrith us to be hurte be which our bliss myte be lesid. And therfore whan the dome is goven and we ben all browte up above, than we cleerly se in God the privities which be now hidde to us. Than shall non of us be stirid to sey in ony wise 'Lord, if it had ben thus, than it had bene full wele'; but we shall seyn al without[273] voice: 'Lord, blissid mot thou ben! For it is thus, it is wele. And now se we verily that all thing is done as it was then ordeynd beforn that onything was made.'

86

The good lord shewid this booke shuld be otherwise performid than at the first writing; and for his werking he will we thus prey, him thankand, trostand, and in him enioyand; and how he made this shewing because he will have it knowen, in which knoweing he will give us grace to love him; for xv yeere after it was answerid that the cause of all this shewing was love, which Ihesus mote grant us. Amen—lxxxvi chapter.

This booke is begunne be Gods gift and his grace, but it is not yet performid, as to my syte. For charite pray we all to God,[274] with Godds werking, thankand, trostand, enioyand; for thus will our good lord be prayd, as be the vnderstonding that I tooke in al his owne mening, and in the swete words wher he seith full merrily 'I am ground of thi beseking'; for trewly I saw and understode in our lords mening that he shewid it for he will have it knowen more than it is, in which knowing he will give us grace to loven him and clevyn to him; for he beholdith his hevenly tresure with so grete love on erth that he will give us more light and solace in hevenly ioy in drawing of our herts, for sorow and merkness which we arn in. And fro that time that it was shewid I desired oftentimes to witten what was our lords mening. And xv yer after and more I was answerid in gostly vnderstonding, seyand thus: 'Woldst thou wetten thi lords mening in this thing? Wete it wele: love was his mening. Who shewid it the? Love. What shewid he the? Love. Wherfore shewid it he? For love. Hold the therin and thou shalt witten and knowen more in the same; but thou shalt never knowen ne witten therein other thing without end.' Thus was I lerid that love was our lords mening. And I saw full sekirly in this and in all, that ere God made us he lovid us; which love was never slakid, no never shall. And in this love he hath don all his werke; and in this love he hath made all things profitable to us; and in this love our life is everlestand. In our making we had beginning; but the love wherin he made us was in him from withoute begynning; in which love we have our beginning. And all this shall be seen in God without end;[275] which Ihesus mot grant us. Amen.

Thus endith the revelation of love of the blissid Trinite shewid by our savior Christ Iesu for our endles comfort and solace, and also to enioyen in him in this passand iorney of this life. Amen, Ihesu, Amen.[276]

I pray almyty God that this booke com not but to the hands of the[m][277] that will be his faithfull lovers, and to those that will submitt them to the feith of holy church and obey the holesom vnderstondyng and teching[278] of the men that be of vertuous life, sadde age and profound lernyng; for this revelation is hey divinitye and hey wisdam, wherfore it may not dwelle with him that is thrall to synne and to the devill. And beware thou take not on thing after thy affection and liking and leve another, for that is the condition of an heretique. But take everything with other and trewly vnderstonden all is according to holy scripture and growndid in the same, and that, Ihesus our very love, light and truth shall shew to all clen soules that with mekenes aske perseverantly this wisdom of hym. And thou, to whome this booke

135

shall come, thanke heyley and hartily our savior Crist Ihesu that he made these shewings and revelations for the, and to the, of his endles love, mercy and goodnes, for thine and our save guide and conduct to everlestyng bliss; the which Ihesus mot grant us. Amen.[279]

INDEX OF REVELATIONS TO CHAPTERS

NOTES

Abbreviations

MS   British Library, Sloane MS No. 2499, copy text for this edition.

P   Paris, Bibliothèque Nationale, MS Fonds Anglais No. 40.
S2   British Library, Sloane Ms No. 3705.

These notes account for the emendations in square brackets in the text and include the more significant variant and additional readings in P and, where relevant S2. (See Introduction p. vii-xi). The variations in chapter divisions between MS and P are also noted here.

1 P adds: for by the same myght wisdom and goodnes that I haue done all this · by the same myght wisdom etc.

2 P well MS wle

3 P xiii

4 P MS omits

5 P adds: for me thought this was not the commune vse of prayer · therfor I sayd lord etc.

6 S2 saying MS sey

7 P MS thes

8 P adds: Thus I toke it for that tyme that our lord Ihesu of his Curteys loue would shewe me comfort before the tyme etc.

9 P MS his

10 P MS omits

11 P MS hedseth

12 P kynde dwellyng

13 P goodnes MS dodeness

14 P knowe oure god verely etc.

15 P adds: A man goyth vppe ryght and the soule of his body is sparyde as a purse fulle feyer · And whan it is tyme of his nescessery it is openyde and sparyde agen fulle honestly · And that it is he · that Doyth this it is schewed ther wher he seyth · he comyth downe to us to the lowest parte of oure nede · For he hath etc.

16 P to MS do

17 P MS they

18 P MS omits

19 P over ȝede

138

20 P MS I saw him sowte

21 P this life

22 P MS omits

23 P full holsomly

24 P his MS is

25 P sowles

26 P seen

27 P ther

28 & 29 P game MS same

30 S2 servants MS servats

31 P same

32 MS xviii

33 P thorow

34 P agyd

35 P askyd MS asky

36 P MS thynyn

37 P MS omits

38 S2 MS omits

39 P adds: seeyng after these ·
other two poyntes whych be
lower. That one is what he
sufferyd. And that other ·
for whom that he sufferyd ·
And etc.

40 P MS wet

41 P be nye (P divides chapter
20 from 21 here but ends 21 at
the same point as MS)

42 S2 The MS he

43 S2 of MS o

44 P MS soyd

45 P thought

46 P bodely MS dodyly

47 nevyr MS neve

48 P And MS Ad

49 S2 two MS tw

50 P she conceyvyd

51 P MS Lodd

52 MS xxviii

53 P sythen

54 P mankynde MS makyd

55 P counceylyd MS counellid

56 P MS sha

57 P fully MS filly

58 P harmes MS harmy

59 P adds: the goodnesse and
the loue of our lorde god
wylle that we wytte that it
shall be. And the myght and
the wysdom of hym by the
same loue wylle heyle it and
hyde it fro vs · what it shalle
be · and how it shall be done ·
And etc.

60 P groundyd MS gowndid

61 P to take prefe of etc.

62 P dampnyd MS dampny

63 P adds: for he wille ther by
· we know trust and beleue
alle that he shalle do · but etc

64 P we may MS me way

65 P adds: oure good lorde
wylle shew vs what it is with
alle etc.

66 P the ende

67 P I hope

68 P hys MS hss

69 P wytt of

70 P hym selfe MS hymsefe

71 P MS omits

72 P hym selfe MS hymsef

73 P MS the

74 S2 known MS kowen

75 P hevynly

76 & 77 P shalle MS sha

78 P lett me aloone my derwurdy etc.

79 P lordys MS Lods

80 P be knowen

81 P MS omits

82 P MS omits

83 P that MS tha

84 P wylle MS millen

85 P as MS a

86 P Peter and paule · Thomas and Iude · Sent Iohn etc.

87 P turned MS turyd

88 S2 underfongyth MS underforgyth P vndertakyth

89 P we

90 P adds: And also whom oure lord wylle · he vysytyth of specialle grace with etc.

91 S2 MS omits

92 P wyllyng MS willy

93 P MS omits

94 P shewed MS sewid

95 P onyd MS ony

96 P febelnes MS febihede

97 P discrecion MS discrtion

98 P MS fifth (the quotation is from the xv revelation chapter 64)

99 P thankyng MS thakyng

100 P MS omits

101 P we

102 P speciall grace

103 P hym selfe MS hymsefe

104 P vnperceyvable MS onpercvable

105 P vnabylnes

106 P MS omits

107 P fulsomly MS fusumly

108 P strengthyth MS stengtneth

109 P MS omits

110 P mystely

111 P kyndly MS kyndy

112 P adds: but in our feyth · And whan we know and see verely and clerely what oure selfe is ÷ than shalle etc.

113 P MS foething

114 P adds: In whych full knowyng we shall verely and clerely know oure god in fulhede etc.

115 P MS in

115 P sympylnesse and vncunnyng

117 P MS omits

118 P mercyfully

119 P MS ageys

120 P oure selfe MS our seffe

121 P come MS cun

122 P knowyng MS kowing

123 P MS the

124 P mayme MS maine

125 P MS and

126 P alle manne

127 P knowyng MS kowing

128 P socurryth

129 P MS omits

130 P adds: that I saw verely
we ought to know and beleue
etc.

131 P all MS a

132 P that MS tha

133 P groundyd MS grounld

134 P that MS tha

135 P lorde MS Lod

136 P MS which

137 P MS now

138 P shall MS sha

139 P lordys MS Lodis

140 P evyn

141 P evyn MS eve

142 P MS pets

143 P new

144 P evyn

145 S2 Mother

146 S2 MS but never it

147 P payne MS payes

148 S2 never MS neve

149 P hath to

150 P there

151 P two MS tw

152 P holy dystroyed

153 P grete MS gre

154 P evyr more MS evemore

155 P orde MS Lod

156 P evyr MS eve

157 P mankynde MS makynd

158 P esy

159 S2 took MS troke

160 P nevyr MS neve

161 P to geder

162 P substaunce MS substane

163 P substance MS substane

164 P kyndnesse

165 P werkyng MS wekyng

166 S2 substance MS subsance

167 P MS omits

168 P MS is

169 P nevyr MS neve

170 P kepyng MS kepid

171 P substaunce MS substane

172 P hym selfe MS hymseffe

173 P kyndely MS kindy

174 P fro without begynning

175 P yeldyng MS reldyng

176 P MS vesyng

177 P oure MS ou

178 P MS omits

179 P adds: Nerest for it is
most of kynd ÷ redyest for it is
most of loue · And sekerest
for etc.

180 P MS omits

181 P MS ix (the quotation
comes from x revelation
chapter 24)

182 P kyndelyth MS kydelyth

183 P strenthyd MS strengtid

184 P nevyr MS neve

185 P flode

186 P it

187 P myght MS my

188 P begynyng MS begynnig

189 P bryng MS byngen

190 P trewly MS sothy

191 P techyth MS tehith

192 P nevyr MS neve

193 P MS foethes

194 P moderhed wylle

195 P other MS othe

196 P divides chapter 63 from 64 here but ends 64 at the same point as MS

197 P no manner of sycknes no etc.

198 P swyft

199 P MS omits

200 P blyneth

201 P MS yf

202 P mercyfulle

203 P evyr

204 P them selfe MS himseffe

205 P MS omits

206 P great MS gre

207 P fulfyllyd MS fufillid

208 P paynes MS peyes

209 P that sawe no more thereof

210 P waxsyd

211 P adds: when I by seaying I raved I shewed my selfe nott to belyue oure lorde god · Nott withstanding I beleft hym truly for the tyme etc.

212 P MS omits

213 P divides chapter 66 from 67 here

214 P chapter 68

215 ʒevyth

216 P adds: The manhode with the godhed syttyth in rest · the godhede rulyth and ʒevyth withoutyn ony instrument or besynesse. And the soule is alle occupyed with the blessyd godhed · that is souereyne myghte etc.

217 & 218 P than MS that

219 P adds: But for he made mannes soule as feyer · as good · as precious as he myght make it a creature therfore the blessyd trynyte is fulle plesyd withoute end in the makyng of mannes soule · And etc.

220 MS omits (P also starts chapter 69 here)

221 P divides chapter 69 from 70 here

222 P there vpon MS therupo

223 P divides chapter 70 from 71 here

224 P blyndnesse MS blinhede

225 S2 glad MS Gad

226 P hath nede

227 P beer

228 P MS ageys

229 P MS Alivaner

230 P marks no division between chapters 71 and 72 but heads the whole section 71

231 P to geder

232 P adds: that is to sey · in his owne lycknes. For etc.

233 S2 sekirnes MS sekirne P feythfulnesse

234 P thyngk MS thyke

235 S2 MS sekernes

236 P also starts chapter 73 here

237 P nevyr MS neve

238 P payne MS peyes

239 P paynes

240 P another MS anothe

241 P whych comyth thorugh lack of true Iugment · and it is agayne etc.

242 P after MS afte

243 P adds: For man that is harde of slepe of synne he etc.

244 P on sonder MS asuder

245 S2 MS omits

246 S2 littlenes

247 P drawyn MS anwin

248 P MS omits

249 P MS to my mynde

250 P MS ageys

251 P MS omits

252 S2 specally MS speially

253 P MS omits

254 P MS omits

255 P MS omits

256 P thy selfe MS selfe

257 P MS omits

258 P he of his curtesy MS he is of his curtesie

259 S2 Love MS lave

260 P MS sweing

261 P te geder

262 S2 wonyth MS wonnyh P dwellyth

263 P MS omits

264 S2 blame

265 P adds: therfore thou arte hevy and sorowfulle · and if thou myghtest lyue without synne etc.

266 P evyr MS eve

267 P MS omits

268 P MS omits

269 S2 medefull MS nedefull

270 P with MS with

271 P MS soft

272 S2 never MS neve

273 P with one

274 P to gedyr

275 P adds: Deo gracias · Explicit liber revelacionum Iulyane anatorite norwyche cuius anime propicietur deus

276 This, with the following passage is attributed to the scribe

277 S2 them MS then

278 S2 teaching MS treching

279 S2 adds: Here end the sublime and wonderful Revelations of the unutterable Loue of God in Iesus Xt, vouchsafed to a Dear Lover of his and in her to all his dear friends and Lovers, whose hearts, like here, do flame in the Loue of our Dearest Iesu.

GLOSSARY

This is not a complete glossary on the text; it is designed to help those who already have some grounding in Middle English. Where words listed occur more than once in the text with the same meaning, spelling variations are noted but only one page reference is given, followed by etc. Variations in meaning are however given separate page references. The arrangement is alphabetical: consonantal i is treated as j and vocalic v with u. It should be noted that g in 'gemeth' and y in 'yeldyng' and 'yemand' represent ʒ. The grammatical abbreviations are self-explanatory.

ablith *pres*. admits 60, *pr.p.*
  ablyng admitting, making accessible 61.
adyten *v*. ordain, prepare 76, *pp*. **adyte** ordained 81 etc.
after that *prep. phr*. according as, to the degree that 63
akynned *pp*. burnt ? scorched 26.
al(l)thing, althyng *pron*. everything 14 etc.
anem(p)ts, a(r)nernst *prep*. concerning, as regards 43 etc.
aperceyvid *pp*. aware, informed 50.
aret *pp*. attributed 74.
assay *n*. experience 100.
assenten *v*. assent 19 etc. *pret*. **as(s)entid assend** assented 74 etc.
as(s)eth, asyeth *n*. satisfaction, reparation 2 etc.
astynten *v*. stop 118.
attemyd *pp*. put down,

subdued 20.
avisement *n*. consideration, reflection 17 etc. clarity and consideration 19.

barme *n*. bosom 119.
beclosyth *pres*. surrounds, encloses 7 etc. *pret*. **beclosid** encircled 14, *pp*. **beclesid, beclosyd** surrounded, enclosed 9 etc.
behoting *vbl.n*. promising 105.
behotist *pres*. promise 123.
behovabil *adj*. expedient, appropriate 38.
bidding *vbl. n*. **bidding of beds** praying with a rosary 112.
blyn *v*. cease 9.
bolned *pp. as adj*. swollen 105.
bolnehede *n*. distension 105.
bouke *n*. trunk of the body 9.
bresten *v*. burst 75, *pret*. **braste** burst 20.

bristinid *pp.* beaten 98.
brynnyt *pres.* burns 123, *pp.*
   brent baked 109.
but if *adv. phr.* unless 13 etc.

charge *n.* burden,
   encumbrance 34, care 79.
chargyn *v.* care, give
   consideration to 55, *pr.p.*
   charging being concerned
   about 29.
che(e)re *n.* expression, manner
   11 etc.
clange, clongen *pp.* wasted
   shrivelled 25.
comenyng *vbl.n.* associating 90.
common *n.* community 100.
conable *adj.* appropriate 20.
curte *n.* court 20.

daggyd *pp.* pierced 25.
daming *pr.p.* cursing 29.
ded(e)ly *adj.* mortal 5 etc.
demyth *pres.* judges 63,
   pp. **demyd** judged 13.
demyng *vbl.n.* judging 18.
discrien *v.* describe 80.
dome *n.* judgement 63 etc.
   pl. **domys** judgements 70.
domysman *n.* one who has
   power to judge, here
   confessor 53
dyte *pret.* arrayed 97,
   pp. **dygte** prepared 77, **dyte**
   ordained 102.

entenden, entendyn *v.* give
   heed to, devote oneself to
   51 etc. *imp.* **entend** devote
   yourself 50, *pret.* **entended**
   paid attention to 51 etc.

entendyng *vbl.n.* concentrating,
   attention 112.
entent *n.* intent 59 etc.
even *adj.* equal, alike 78. even,
   evin, evyn cristen fellow
   christian(s) 10 etc.
evenforth *adv.* straight ahead
   4, **even lyke** equally alike
   32, **even ryte/ryth** directly
   80, righteously 109.
evese, evys *n.pl.* eaves 10.
evisid *pp.* cut 108.
evyl *adv.* wretchedly, painfully
   20.

faylen *v.* fail, die 27, *pres.* **us**
   faylyth fails in us 60, **feilith**
   nougte nothing is wanting
   18, *pret.* **faledyn** failed 27,
   faylid died 27, *pr.p.* **faylyng**
   failing 60.
fele *adj.* many, excellent 9,
   excellent 50.
forbetyth *pres.* beats severely
   53.
fordreth *pres.* assists, helps
   103, *pr.p.* **fortheryng** helping
   64.
fornempts *adv.* next, before
   even fornempts right before
   76.
for(th)with *adv.* at once 59
   etc.
freisly *adv.* freely 5.
ful(l)hede *n.* completeness 9
   etc. **of fulhede** *adv. phr.*
   abundantly, fully 89.

gemeth *pres.* takes care of 109.
   pr.p. **yemand** caring for 82.
glode *pret..* glided 105.

go(o)dhede *n.* goodness 91 etc.

grutchin *pres* grudge, complain 82.

gru(t)ching *vbl.n.* complaining, grumbling 29 etc.

halseth, halsith *pres.* embraces 7 etc.

hame *n.* outer covering, coating 15.

harre *adj.* keen 24.

hend(e) *adj.* courteous, gracious 17 etc.

hevyed *pret.* grieved 108.

heyhede *n.* sublimity 90.

heyly *adj.* sublime, glorious 49 etc.

heynen *v.* raise, exalt 40, *pret.* **heyned** raised 42.

holehede *n.* completeness, wholeness 56.

impropried *pp.* assigned 96.

inderly *adv.* earnestly 57, heartily 108.

iangelyng *vbl.n.* chattering, gossiping 112.

ianglyd *pret.* chattered 112.

lak *n.* fault, offence 39 etc.

lakid *pp.* disparaged 39.

lauhen, lavhyn, lawhyn *v.* laugh 21 etc. *pret.* **lavhyd, leuhe** laughed 21 etc.

lavhyng *vbl.n.* laughing 21.

lenehede *n.* emaciation 15.

leryd *pret.* taught 40, learnt 48, *pp.* **lerid** taught 36 etc.

leryd *pp. as n.* the taught 47.

leryng *vbl.n.* learning, instruction 45 etc.

lettyn *v.* stop 44, *pres.* **lettyth** stops 54 etc. *pret.* **letted, lettyd** stopped, prevented 38 etc. *pp.* **lettid** prevented 38.

lever *comp.adv.* rather 22.

levyth *pres* bestows 39.

lightening *vbl.n.* enlightenment 1.

likenes *n.* comparison 9 etc.

likyng, lekyng *vbl.n.* liking, enjoying 23 etc. *as adj.* 24, *as adv.* 22.

lulshed *n.* littleness, insignificance 120.

lyken, lekyn *v.* like 33 etc. *pres.* **lekyt, likyth** likes 60, 61 etc. *pret.* **lekyd** liked 77.

mekin *v.* humble 77.

mene *n.* means, intermediary, mediator 5 etc. *pl.* **menys** 8 etc.

mene *adj.* intermediary 89.

namely *adv.* especially 5 etc.

neyghen *v.* draw near to 124.

nowten, nowtyn *v.* set at nought 7 etc. *pp.* **nawted, nowted, nowtid** set at nought 7 etc. **nowted of** stripped, divested 7 etc.

nowtyng *vbl.n.* setting at nought, despising 38 etc.

onde *n.* breath 5.

one *v.* unite, make one with 126. *pres.* **onyth** joins, unites 60 etc. *pp.* **onyd** united 7 etc.

onethis, onethys *adv.* scarcely 5 etc.

onperceyvable *adj.* imperceptible, indiscernible 61.

onyng *vbl.n.* uniting, union 27 etc.

otherwhile *adv.* sometimes 53.

overrede *pret.refl.* override, fig. overspread 14.

overleyd *pp.* overcome 66.

paid, payd *pp.* pleased, satisfied 31 etc.

partie *adv.* openly 11.

parties *n.pl.* parts, various facets 63.

passible *adj.* capable of suffering 30, negative **un/on-passible** 42 etc.

pellots *n.pl.* pellets, globes 10.

pesid *pp.* at peace 44 etc.

quave *n.* quagmire 105.

rapyd *pp.* beaten 39.

redy *adj.* red 24.

reprovid, reprovyd *adj. as n.* the reprobate, depraved 21 etc.

reulihede *n.* pitifulness, wretchedness 15.

reuly *adj.*wretchedly 16.

reward, in reward of *prep.phr.* in comparison with 4 etc. also **in reward that** 66, **no reward to** *prep.phr.* no regard to 33 etc.

ronkyllid *pp.* festered 26.

rythwis *adj.* righteous 60.

se, see *n.* dwelling place, city 88 etc.

see-ground *n.* sea-bed 15.

seker, sekir *adj.* sure 28 etc. fulsekird very sure 17.

sekir, sekirly *adv.* surely 18 etc.

sekirnes(s) *n.* sureness 23 etc.

semelant *n.* appearance 108.

seming *vbl.n.* furrowing (ie. weals) 19.

semyd *pret.* pressed **semyd of** sagged from 26.

semys *n.* weals 33.

sharpely *adv.* swiftly 105.

shrewd *adj.* evil, malignant 108, **shrewid** grievous 124.

shrewidnes *n.* wickedness 21.

slade *n.* valley, boggy place 72 etc.

slakid *pp* weakened, diminished 135.

slyppe *n.* wet clay 85.

sperid *pp.* closed 41 etc.

stede *n.* place 59 etc.

steknes *n.pl.* speckles 108.

steyte, streyte *adj.* tight 76 etc.

steytehede *n.* tightness 79.

stondyng *adv.* considering 15, *prep.* 45 etc.

stonyed *pp.* stunned 73 etc.

sweeme *n.* sorrow 4 etc.

swem(e)ly, swemefully *adv.* sorrowfully 15 etc.

sweming *vbl.n.* grieving 129.

sweppys *n.pl.* scourges, whips 80.

swinkin *v.* toil, labour 77.

syde *adj.* ample 75 etc.

syte *n.* city 109.

than *adv.* when 108, **than saw I no more thereof** when I no longer saw anything of (the shewings.)

thounys *n.pl.* temples 108.

tilestone *n.* brick 108.

therewhiles *adv.* in that time 15.

vggyng *n.* horror 28.
vnderfongyn *v.* receive 3 etc. *pres.* underfongyth receives 53.
unethes see **onethis**
unornely *adv.* plainly 81.

vernacle *n.* the cloth imprinted with the image of Christ's face, attributed to St Veronica 12.

ward *n.* place of protection 75.
wrangyng *pr.p.* wringing 25.
wretches *n.pl.* desires of vengeance, spites 69.

yeldyng *vbl.n.* recompensing 94 etc.
yemand see **gemeth.**